Oh Oh, Daddy's Cooking!

A Father's Method of Feeding His "Tribe"

TED W. PAROD

Publisher's Cataloging in Publication Data
Parod, Ted W.
Oh Oh, Daddy's Cooking!/by Ted W. Parod
1. Cookery
2. Cookery, American
641.512   LC 91-75372
ISBN 0-9627432-4-0:$9.95 Softcover GBC

Cover Design by Mark Woodruff

Illustrations by Leslie Parod and Mark Woodruff

Manufactured in the United States of America

Published by Echo Lake Press
P.O. Box 23175, Phoenix, Arizona 85063

Band-Aid® is a trademark of Johnson & Johnson

Bisquick™ is a trademark of General Mills, Inc.

Golden Mushroom™ is a trademark of Campbell Soup Co.

Kleenex® is a trademark of Kimberly-Clark Corp.

Miracle Whip™ is a trademark of Kraft, Inc.

Scotch™ Tape is a trademark of 3M Corporation.

TO MY FAMILY

INTRODUCTION

T hroughout this cookbook I use the words "Old Indian Recipes." Actually, nothing in this book is derived from anything either old or Indian. When my first child reached the age of 22 months, it became apparent that I would have to use deception when she asked what I was cooking. I had never bothered to name the stuff that I made. I just mixed together whatever was on hand and served it. It was just "stuff" that tasted pretty good. If it happened to look and taste like something that people had seen before, so much the better.

My daughter, however, had demanded a name for the stuff or she wouldn't eat it. Being relatively quick of wit on occasion, I told her that it was an "Old Indian" recipe handed down to me by Chief Dirty Face of the Mucky-Muck tribe. That seemed to satisfy her and at the same time start a family tradition. As each succeeding child was born and grew older, the same questions were asked and the same answers were given. EVERYTHING I cooked was an "Old Indian" recipe and remains so to this day.

Ever since I was a kid I have liked to cook. I started by simply mixing together things that sounded good and then eating the results, if possible. Since this technique worked pretty well for me when I was four or five years old, I stuck with it until adulthood when I discovered that people actually wrote ingredients down and referred to "cookbooks" for other people's ideas. Gone was the spontaneity and creativity of cooking, but then again, so were the bloopers and blunders.

Having discovered "cookbooks" and actually reading several of them, I have rejected most as being too precise and lacking in imagination. A quarter teaspoon of this, a tablespoon of that, a number 2 can of something else, exactly 2½ cups of "sifted" flour, and the stuff still doesn't taste like it should or look like the picture. Well, in this cookbook, precise amounts of ingredients, or, for that matter, the ingredients themselves, are really not that important.

If the recipe calls for a half a cup of something and you dump in a whole cup, don't worry about it — it will taste just as good. The same holds true for seasonings (I like lots of seasonings as they tend to cover up a multitude of sins). If the recipe calls for X amount of salt, and you don't like salt, simply don't put it in. If it calls for hot sauce, and you don't like hot sauce, don't put as much or ANY in. It really won't affect the outcome of the recipe all that much. This allows you a great deal of latitude and creativity while still "conforming" to a time-tested recipe. In keeping with this philosophy, there are no pictures in this book to embarrass or shame you. What your creation looks like when done is what it is SUPPOSED to look like. With THIS cookbook you never have to feel inferior.

Since I came from the school of "if it can't be cooked on high, it's not worth cooking," temperature settings are of little consequence unless specified. "High" simply means that you have to stir faster to keep the stuff from burning — so suit yourself. Over the years, however, I have discovered that stoves have settings other than "high" and that wives have a tendency to become irritated when the bottoms of their expensive pans become permanently warped (they don't make them like they used to). Coincidental with these discoveries came remarkable improvements in both my cooking and my domestic relations.

In spite of this progress, my wife tends to display odd behavior when the kids and I enter the kitchen with a new "Old Indian" recipe to test. She gets that funny little look on her face — sort of a cross between apprehension and fear — and then quickly snatches up her favorite appliances and utensils and scurries off with them. No doubt this flurry of humorous activity is designed to test my growing ability to create delightful meals with a minimum of equipment. Her thoughtfulness has been a boon to me in designing many of my famous "one pan" (warped, of course) "Old Indian" recipes.

With few exceptions (all duly noted), every recipe in this cookbook was created by me. However, a quick trip to the Library of Congress will establish that at least 500 million cookbooks, each containing approximately 65 recipes, have been published in this country alone. For each of these published recipes there exists in the unpublished hearts, minds, and shoeboxes of American women, at least 20 or 30 similar recipes. After all, you can do only so much with a dead chicken. Therefore, if one of my recipes sounds familiar or looks like the one Aunt Maude gave you, I apologize and hereby give you and your Aunt all the credit.

The purpose of this book is not to tout the originality of my own creations, but rather, to persuade fathers that kitchens and kids are a lot of fun and not at all mysterious. A little common sense can cut right through those thinly veiled enigmas known as "cooking" and "raising kids."

Don't get carried away with the common sense thing tho, as it usually doesn't enhance man's understanding of women. That's a whole nuther area of confusion that doesn't respond well to logic.

Years of living with women and children has produced in me a large pool of knowledge about the behavoir patterns of this group, particularly when subject to specific stimuli such as everyday life. For the new husband/father and even the experienced husband/father who has not bothered to question traditional child raising techniques, or why women sometimes act in perplexing ways, this book may, in so far as possible, shed some light on these mysteries. Besides, you should spend some time with your kids while they are in the "Daddy can do anything" stage and before they reach the "Daddy's a jerk" stage.

The pages that follow are filled with hints, tips, a little insight, and darn good "Old Indian" recipes. Lots of sins have been committed in writing this book. For instance, among those who "talk cooking" (as opposed to doing it), you don't "top with," you "garnish with"; you don't use "onions," you use "shallots" (whatever they are). Nevertheless, the recipes have been tested with great success on my kids, unsuspecting relatives, and the neighborhood dogs. No deaths have occurred. The neighbors' pets, by the way, can provide an excellent source of critique. If they eat your creation readily, don't regurgitate, and show no signs of gastro-intestinal distress within three hours, you probably have a winner.

8

TABLE OF CONTENTS

Section One
Kids, Women and Other Curiosities

Section Two
"Old Indian" Recipes

Section One

Kids, Women and Other Curiosities

KIDS

For those of you who do not have them, kids (also known as children) are small people that generally own big people. Basically, American kids sleep when they are tired, eat when they are hungry, watch lots of television, have very little responsibility, and own $700,000 worth of toys. All big people want to become kids as soon as they can afford it.

Children are living contradictions and, therefore, a constant source of bewilderment for their parents. For example, most kids have extremely good hearing but are deaf. Whisper about a child who is in his/her room behind closed doors listening to a stereo with the volume control set on "earthquake" and the kid hears every word you say. Call the same kid at the top of your lungs to do the dishes and he goes deaf. All kids are extremely intelligent and very dumb. My three-year old son, Atilla-the-Hun, is perfectly capable of disassembling my car but unable to pick up toys and put them in the toy box. My eight-year old daughter can program the VCR and boot up the computer but can't figure out how to make her bed.

To further heighten parents' bewilderment over the "smart/dumb" dichotomy, male children eventually settle on one or the other (stupid or smart) as they grow older, but female children usually carry the smart/dumb trait into adulthood. My wife, who is one of the most intelligent people that I have ever met (male or female) can overhaul a vacuum cleaner with a bobby pin or calculate the price per ounce of a 5 lb. bag of flour to the hundredth of a cent in less than half a second. This is the same woman who will drive across town like a bat-out-of-hell to tell me that the red oil pressure light won't go out after she starts the car.

Kids are marvelous little creatures that learn fast and, in spite of what we might think, cannot be fooled for very long. When one kid figures something out (like the Easter Bunny) all kids within a four square mile area reach the same conclusion simultaneously. I think it's done by osmosis.

Kids are the only ones of God's creatures that can have lawns to mow, beds to make, dishes to wash, thousands of toys to play with, TV to watch, computer games to play, homework to do, bikes to ride, parents to bug, books to read, etc., and still have "nothing to do." Basically, the more the kid has to do, the more he/she has "nothing to do." This phenomenon becomes more pronounced as your children grow older. There is absolutely nothing you can do to alleviate this situation, so don't court frustration by even trying.

HOW TO GET YOUR KIDS TO EAT

Method #1 – Starvation

I find this to be the most effective method of inducing children of all ages and temperament to down quantities of questionable food and even compliment the "chef." By "starvation," I don't mean the kind found in Bangladesh or Africa, but a much more subtle type. A little knowledge lets you pull this off quite nicely. Kids are as much creatures of habit as adults are and their tummies start rumbling about mealtime, whenever that may be. Therefore, deny the youngsters any form of snack or in-between-meal goodies (except water) before lunch or dinner. Blame anything and anyone but yourself for this denial ("Your mother said not to let you eat between meals," or "It's national weight-loss day," etc.)

Next, put off fixing the actual meal for at least an hour by craftily appearing to be busy planning the menu. By now you should have ravenous children on your hands, children who will eat even YOUR cooking. If you manage to prolong the meal long enough, the kids will not only eat the stuff, but will probably tell others what a wonderful cook daddy is. With children under twelve, this system is foolproof and will ensure your reputation as an "Old Indian" cook par excellence.

Teenagers, on the other hand, are ALWAYS hungry and will continuously consume anything resembling food PROVIDED that said food is neither nutritious nor generally "good for you." Greasy hamburgers with fries and cholesterol-soaked pizzas top the list, while anything healthful is frowned upon as "dinner." In pursuing the "starvation technique," these older children may require physical restraint and will probably have to be bound and gagged. This in no way detracts from the effectiveness of the system.

Method #2 – Threats

While it is probably against the law in all 50 states to threaten your children with bodily harm for not eating their food, there are several other partially effective threats one can use without running afoul of the local constabulary. Chief among them is your power to turn young children into frogs. This worked pretty well with my first four kids but lost some of its oomph with my fifth child, "Ralph." Actually, it worked fairly well with her, too, until she began to realize that I either couldn't, or wouldn't, turn her into a frog (or the other kids squealed). She completely ignored my threats.

Craftily, I switched to my next sure-fire threat and told her that if she didn't eat whatever it was that I put in front of her that I would unhook her belly button and her legs would fall off. This lasted until she reached the age of reason and began to get my number (about 22 months old), at which time she just smiled at me sweetly and said "Oh, Daddy, you wouldn't do that!" I suspect that the other kids had a talk with her, particularly my three year old who takes vicious delight in undermining my status as an authority figure not to be messed with. Nevertheless, I find that threats can be reasonably effective on younger children PROVIDING that the little brats don't conspire against you.

My eldest daughter, "Button" (the nag), who is 8-going-on-28, seems to represent the outer age limits whereby kids will respond favorably to intimidation or ominous threats. There is, however, an exception to this general age rule, a nifty technique discovered by my neighbor, The Grump, who simply threatened to sell his children into slavery. He steadfastly declares that it works well into the early teenage years when, with cars to wash, lawns to mow, dishes to do, floors to vacuum, and beds to be made, the kids suddenly think that they are slaves anyway! This occurs about the time their biological clock takes over and they a) become lazy bums, and b) will eat anything anyway.

Method #3 – Conspiracy

Bring the kids into your confidence. If they help prepare your "Old Indian" recipes, they somehow feel that they have to eat it. I've watched my kids gag down stuff that would choke a junk yard dog just because they helped make it. This is a rather sneaky technique, but it works, unless of course, you have a particularly honest kid who, like my seven year old daughter, "Squirt," is fond of saying things like "Dad, this is AWFUL," or "Barf city, Dad, barf city." Try not to let these little kill-joys dampen your enthusiasm for cooking by remembering that their taste buds probably haven't fully developed yet. The fact that this particular kid will eat stewed tomatoes and liver is further proof that she is not a reliable food critic.

How do you know when a kid is old enough to work with you in the kitchen? Simple. There will come a time when each child questions the integrity of the stuff that you create. THAT is the time to bring him or her into your confidence and introduce them to the wonders of "Old Indian" cooking.

Remember, secrecy is a big part of this marvelous ploy. Just select one ingredient from your "Old Indian" recipe and declare it a "secret" handed down to you by old Chief So-and-So. It really doesn't matter what part of the recipe that you choose. For instance, with mashed potatoes, it could be the potatoes themselves. This will drive your wife crazy. Once she tastes the stuff and declares it fit for human consumption, your fellow conspirators will gleefully state that it contains a secret "Old Indian" ingredient known only to them and their dad. This is particularly effective with something like instant mashed potatoes where she can't figure out why they taste so "normal." She may even begin lurking around the kitchen when you and the kids are "creating." This is good as it means that your stature as an "Old Indian" cook has been greatly enhanced.

HOW TO CUT THE COSTS OF FEEDING A FAMILY

A note of caution is definitely in order. Most parents go through life sacrificing for their kids. This is ridiculous as they don't appreciate it anyway. Giving a six-year old kid part (or all) of your T-bone steak is akin to pouring a fine Chateau Lafite down the throat of a wino. Kids prefer hot dogs to steak anyway UNLESS you train them otherwise. Therefore, never give kids steak or lobster (or anything else that is expensive and that you like). DO NOT assist the little monsters in cultivating a taste for high-priced food early in life, i.e., while they are still living with you.

Kids will eventually develop a taste for the more expensive items heretofore reserved for "Daddy" (want to see a 16 oz. jar of imported olives disappear in one meal?) Postponing this inevitable day as long as possible will add considerably to your standard of living. I actually know of people who retired wealthy by contributing to their investment portfolio rather than indulging their children's expensive culinary tastes when young. In order to do this you will have to resort to tactics that in any other situation would be socially unacceptable, like B.O.

Tactic #1 – Lie!

Tell them that their systems haven't matured enough to handle steak, lobster, etc. Tell them anything, even that the food is unhealthy and that you are only eating it to prevent them from getting sick.

Tactic #2 – Describe The Food In Graphic Detail.

Steak now becomes "the flesh from a dead cow." You can enhance the effect by hanging pictures of cute little cows with big brown eyes around the dining room. Buy your kids soft little stuffed Cows to curl up with. This rotten trick is especially effective with female children.

Tactic #3 – Deception.

Have them taste a piece of gristle and lead them to believe that the entire steak is that way. The same with lobster. Give them a little piece of inedible claw to fool with and tell them that it takes years to learn how to extract meat from it. (It does anyway.)

Tactic #4 – Concealment.

Hide the gourmet (expensive) items, like imported olives, smoked oysters, etc., where they would never look — with the dish soap, scrub buckets, and vacuum cleaner.

With a little imagination, you can come up with a lot of other neat ideas to keep the kids away from chicken breasts and allow you to better protect your epicurean interests from intrusion. Just remember to start when the little munchkins are young, and ALWAYS be on the lookout for good hiding places.

MYTHS CONCERNING WOMEN AND CHILDREN

Myth #1

Women have eyes in the back of their heads. That's ridiculous. Women do not have eyes in the back of their heads. They have radar. On numerous occasions I have watched my wife's reaction when one of the kids announced his or her presence in the house by slamming the door. Even tho she might be in a different room, she instantly and unerringly identifies the child and issues the appropriate command: "Bumper, wipe your feet before you track mud through the house." (How did she know the kid was playing with the garden hose?) Or, "Shandy, take that frog out of your pocket before you come in this house." Or even more mysterious, "Katie, you and your friend will have to play in your room until I finish cleaning." etc. How do women DO that without seeing the actual kid(s)? Nobody seems to know for sure, but I suspect it has something to do with hormones.

Myth #2

Children can be cleaned and kept clean. This is pure bunk. It's a kid's JOB to get dirty. Besides, it is anatomically impossible for a kid to remain clean for more than 10 minutes. Some scholars say four or five minutes is the maximum "clean period" that parents can reasonably expect from their kids. No amount of threats, bribery, exhortation, or even isolation, will extend this period.

The average kid is designed to be dirty. On close observation, one will note that kids have short legs, thus putting them closer to the ground and all the things on it — weeds, mud, squashed bugs, and dirt, to name a few. Chubby little hands are cleverly designed to spill whole glasses of red juice down the front of clean white dresses, and rather small mouths will not accept the large pieces of chocolate cake that kids try to shove in (before brother, sister, or family dog gets it). Most normal children have arms that are seven feet long. Therefore, anything that is placed "out of reach" on a counter, table, or shelf, will eventually wind up on the kid.

I once experimented with my eldest son "Bumper" when he was only two years old by cleaning him thoroughly and locking him in an absolutely sterile room — no food, dirt, or anything that would rub off. When I opened the door fifteen minutes later, I found him sitting in the middle of the floor, grinning at me. Gum was in his hair, chocolate cake was smeared on his face, egg yolk on his clothes, brown furniture polish on his hands, and mud on his feet.

Impossible? Not at all. I have talked to dozens of parents who have experienced the same thing. Kids will be kids, and part of being a kid is getting dirty. In a kid's world, being "clean" is socially unacceptable. A father should not worry about his children being squeaky clean unless he can't distinguish them from his wife's floral settee or the kids blend in with the garbage. Due to the presence of mothers, however, this condition rarely occurs. See Myth #3.

Myth #3

Children should be frequently cleaned. This is not only futile, but utter nonsense. A "recently cleaned" kid is good enough for most fathers, but many mothers are like ovens and have a "continuous clean" cycle. They are constantly cleaning things around the house and rubbing stuff off the kids. It seems like whenever they have nothing else to do, they grab the nearest kid and start cleaning. Even in public, mothers can't seem to help themselves. They have this disgusting habit of wetting the end of a handkerchief or napkin with the tip of their tonque and then rubbing some imaginary spot off their child, causing little red marks to appear on the kid's face. In any family restaurant you can see dozens of kids with little red marks on their faces. I suspect that women would gleefully rub little red marks on other mother's kids if it were allowed.

I once watched my wife stare at a man and his son having breakfast at a table across from us in a family restaurant. She couldn't take her eyes off a little piece of egg on the kid's chin. After a while she became increasingly nervous and irritable and, on several occasions, unconsciously picked up a napkin and wet it with the tip of her tongue. I noticed several other women acting in the same agitated manner as my wife. They reminded me of drug addicts going through withdrawal. When they got up to leave, I noticed that the man's son was the only kid in the place without little red marks on his face.

It is not necessary to clean kids as frequently as women do to prevent the child from becoming rancid. Baths every other day should prevent anything on the child from taking root. Besides, the enamel on bathtubs will usually last longer if spared the abrasive compounds normally carried on young children.

Having five kids of my own, I have devised a method of periodically cleaning them with a garden hose and broom. A few hands full of laundry detergent, lots of squealing, giggling, and laughter, and they usually come out squeaky clean. Kids drip dry very well. I suggest that you try this method, but watch out for your wife. Mothers tend to frown on this procedure as it doesn't involve bathtubs or handkerchiefs with spit on them.

KEEPING KIDS CLEAN DURING MEALS

Mothers are always wiping on kids while they eat. This doesn't make sense as they just get more food on themselves — the younger they are, the more food. Fathers should wait until the meal is over and THEN clean the kid. I suspect that there is a biological reason for kids getting food on themselves. Food nourishes the skin and makes it nice and soft — note the softness of a baby's skin and compare it to the progressive deterioration of children's and adults' skin as they grow older and progressively neater. Women have been washing their own faces for centuries with every cleaner known to mankind and still they get wrinkles. Kids don't. And in a brilliant fit of inconsistency what do women put on their faces when they want to get rid of the wrinkles? FOOD. The same things that they wiped off the faces of their children while the poor kids were trying to eat: oatmeal, egg, cucumber, and even mud!

I bring this to your attention merely to show that it is unnecessary, and probably harmful, to wash or wipe on a kid during meals. As a rule of thumb, only 10% of the food served to a young child gets inside. The other 90% winds up on the face, hands, arms, and in the hair. This is perfectly normal, and, as previously stated, is probably nature's way of ensuring healthy skin and hair while at the same time not over-feeding the child. Even as the youngster gets older only a small percentage of food actually makes it to the interior of the kid. The rest of it is used as a sort of body armor to ward off mosquitos and evil spirits. Female children will become progressively cleaner until they reach their "neatness zenith" sometime during the late teenage years. Male children remain basically filthy until they discover girls.

This is the natural way of things, so don't fight it. Fathers should not try to keep their kids clean during feeding time but should wait until the little monsters are through eating, as evidenced by the very young ones spitting out food and the older ones playing in it. Now is the time to clean — women use little paper wipey things and wash cloths, but modern fathers use modern tools. That's why the manufacturers put those neat little spray nozzles in sinks.

For the more heavily soiled child, there is always the garden hose. Because this method is quick, easy, and the kids enjoy it, mothers tend to frown on its use and sometimes get a little testy, therefore, fathers should not use this technique in the immediate presence of mothers but should let them wash each squirming child with cloth and little pieces of paper that smell good. Note the look of disgust on the kid's face and notice the smile on the mother's. This should tell you something. The mother is getting even with the kid for having nice skin and "baby soft" hair.

CHILDREN'S NAMES

At this point, one should remember that most kids have two names — a real name and a "hollering at" name. I give women 100% of the credit for inventing and developing to a fine degree the "hollering at" name. My children, for example, have REAL names like Bumper, Shandy, Button, Squirt, and for my littlest daughter, Ralph. These real names serve our kids with dignity and decorum throughout their ever expanding world. They answer to their real names, call each other by their real names, and are known throughout the neighborhood by their real names. There are no slurs, inuendo, hidden meanings, or thinly veiled threats attached to the use of their real names. They live in a friendly little world where everyone knows and uses their proper REAL names.

It is only when their mother (a woman) stands at the back door and hollers "DANIEL WAYNE PAROD (Bumper), GET IN HERE THIS INSTANT," that their little world is suddenly thrown into chaos. Most children will react differently from each other, but it is always negative — the hackles stand up on the backs of the kids' necks, some cower and slink towards the menacing voice, while others (me included) hide.

I think the world would be a far better place if mothers had not invented the "hollering at" name and saddled their offspring with it for the rest of their lives. Pause for a moment and reflect: Do you really think Adolf Hitler would have risen to a position of infamy if his name had remained "Dolfy"? Of course not! And how about Benito Mussolini? Do you think for one minute that this Fascist could have become the Premier and dictator of Italy if his real name, "Mussy," had been used instead of his "hollering at" one? No way! He wouldn't have received two votes between snickers. The world could have been spared a lot of anguish if mothers had paid a little more attention to the way fathers name their kids.

On a more positive note, take a look at the effects of "real" names on universal peace and happiness. Start with Russia, the Evil Empire, as ex-president Reagan called it, a repressive government and world threat if there ever was one. Along comes "Gorby," and the winds of change begin to blow. A measure of democracy and freedom of the press begin to creep in, the military as well as militant policy are deemphasized and the world starts to breathe a little easier. The people of western AND eastern civilized countries seem to love him. Could this have happened if the media and his followers knew him only by his "hollering at" name of Mikhail Gorbachev?

And how about Dwight D. Eisenhower? With a name like that, he HAD to join the military, but the presidency? No sir, not until he started using his "real" name, "Ike." It was "Ike" who was elected president, not Dwight D. Eisenhower. The campaign buttons proudly proclaimed "I like Ike," and "Vote for Ike." Why, you can't even FIT Dwight D. Eisenhower on a campaign button!

I think by now that you get my point. Rather than belabor the issue, it would suffice to say that some of the world's ills would cease to exist if more people used their real names instead of their formal "hollering at" names given to them by their mothers. Fathers, of course, never have to resort to this vicious use of formal nomenclature — due to their superior understanding of children's minds.

As each of us grows a little older, we realize that there are many things that men should not do. We should not endanger our lives without good reason, we should not scrub too much on our kids or use their "hollering at" names, but above all, we should stay away from certain domestic obligations such as "going to the store for your wife." Why? Read on.

GOING-TO-THE-STORE-FOR-YOUR-WIFE

This is to be avoided at all costs. Most of the time, women don't really need the stuff they send us to the store for. They do it just to assure themselves that we're still dumb. Whatever we bring home will be wrong. They start with something simple like "bring home a gallon of milk." Well, it turns out that cows don't make plain old milk anymore. They make "whole milk" (as if they could make "part milk"), "2% milk," "1% milk," and a watery substance called "skim milk." If you bring home the "whole milk," she'll make some comment about it being unhealthy or not good for you. If you bring home "skim milk," it's too watery and "we never use it."

The same basic thing holds true for bread. NOBODY makes plain old bread anymore. There are at least 400 kinds of bread in the average supermarket and no matter what kind or size you bring home, it will be wrong. Your best bet is to simply select the kind you think is the most interesting. When you get home, just give her your best "steely-eyed" look, hand her the loaf and say "We were lucky this time. There's been a run

28

on bread and this was the last loaf left in the entire store. I had to run over seven women with my shopping cart to get it." Then square your shoulders and walk away. You have effectively torpedoed her prepared comments about your incompetence and injected an element of uncertainty in her thinking. This is good.

"Going-to-the-store-for-your-wife" can leave you permanently confused. For instance, you are asked (told) to go to the store and get a box of something (laundry detergent, breakfast cereal, etc). Craftily you ask "what size?" She says "large." Pretty simple, right? Wrong! You see, manufacturers don't make "large" anymore (in the descriptive sense), AND SHE KNOWS IT. They make "giant," "huge," "economy," "family," "super," and "institutional" sizes, but "large" is actually small and tucked away somewhere with the "trial," "sample," and "travel" sizes in a corner. If you take the small "large" box home will your wife be happy or did she really mean "large" in the sense of the institutional 20 lb. size?

Shopping by description is not the way to do it. Instead, go to the store and squarely face the array of boxes. Disregard the size description on the box and simply choose one that either a) looks familiar, or b) appears to contain enough for your family's use. Bear in mind that these boxes are only half full anyway, ostensibly due to "settling" or "compaction during shipping," but most likely due to collusion with the box manufacturers. It really makes little difference tho as it will always be the wrong size when you get it home.

This system, where "large" actually means small and "economy" means expensive, was designed by the same clear-thinking genius responsible for women's dress sizes. In this system, there are "junior," "misses," "womens," "large women," "full," "petite" and "half" (?) sizes. My wife, who, like other women, pretends to actually understand this system, takes a size 8 "misses" OR a size 9 "junior," OR a size 8 "womens." She contends that this system allows women to purchase clothing that will precisely fit their figures (until they get the stuff home, where it becomes too small). Men should understand that these systems cannot be understood, and therefore, should not even try. To do so is to risk dire consequences.

I once knew a man who was married to the same woman for forty years and who was guilty of frequently "Going-to-the-store-for-his-wife." This kindly, if somewhat befuddled, old gentleman had a heart condition for which he took medication. His doctor told him that if he experienced chest pains that he was to take a somewhat "larger" dose of his medication. Of course, after forty years of marriage, "larger" came to mean "smaller" and the poor old guy kept taking less and less of his medication and finally died. His buddies were saddened to hear of his death but could understand how it happened.

If you DO occasionally bring the right thing home from the store, your wife will suspect that you are beginning to understand "the system." This, of course, cannot be tolerated and she will introduce a new element designed to humble and humiliate you — THE COUPON.

The coupon, ostensibly a money-saving device, is really part of a diabolical plot between wives, checkout clerks, and manufacturers. The purpose of this plot is to keep husbands from becoming too familiar with "the system." True understanding of coupon use cannot be attained by men because its inner workings are shrouded in secrecy.

What little we know about it involves a pagan ritual of mutilating magazines and newspapers, and a few token women who actually "use" coupons. This "use" of coupons is an elaborate sham designed to convince men that coupons have a purpose other than contributing to the confusion of husbands and fathers. In reality, only about 2% of all coupons printed are actually used. This 2% represents those given to husbands to "Go-to-the-store-for-your-wife" with.

As far as I can determine, this is how the coupon plot works: first, women enter an altered state of consciousness known as "coupon frenzy" whereby magazines and newspapers are chopped-up for their coupon content. Then the coupons are filed away in various boxes, put in purses, and stuffed behind the breadbox. Next, the coupons are allowed to "age" for various periods of time after which most of them are thrown away for being "out of date." The remaining coupons are then given to husbands for use on certain days at particular stores across town. The selected store must be one that can be reached only after a minimum 30 minute drive through heavy traffic. This particular store will "double" your 20 cent coupon, thereby substantially reducing the twelve dollar gasoline cost of getting there — but only on Wednesdays.

Now you come in contact with the third member of the coupon triad — the checkout clerk. This is the person whose job it is to embarrass you in front of all the women in the store. After standing for 30 minutes in a line marked "EXPRESS LANE – 300 ITEMS OR LESS – CASH ONLY," you present your item and the coupon to a checkout clerk named "Barb." (All "express lane – 300 items or less – cash only" checkout clerks are named "Barb.")

"Barb" will stare at both you and your coupon with disgust and say "You can't use that coupon in this line." Half the women in the store are now staring at you as Barb calls the manager over and explains in a loud voice how you have defiled the sanctity of the "EXPRESS LANE–300 ITEMS OR LESS–CASH ONLY" line with your coupon. Whereupon the manager will

look at you with horror for a few long moments before announcing in a sarcastic voice that you will have to use a "regular" checkout lane. This allows time for word to spread throughout the store about your travesty and for the rest of the women in the checkout lines to mutter and buzz amongst themselves while they stare at you. This is not all bad, because while they're watching you slink to the back of a "regular" checkout line, the three guys who were standing behind you in the "EXPRESS LANE–300 ITEMS OR LESS–CASH ONLY" line, were able to sneak out of the store after quickly swallowing their coupons.

Arriving at the head of the "regular" line after only 2 hrs. and 10 minutes of waiting amongst shopping carts filled with screaming kids with little red marks on their faces and a few groceries, the clerk will inform you that your coupon is only good for the 15.6 oz. "economy size" and not for the 15.4 oz. "family size" that you have. This, of course, means that you have to make your way back through the crowd of staring women and screaming children with little red marks on their faces to get the right size for your coupon.

On again reaching the checkout clerk after only 3 hrs. and 20 minutes in the "regular" line and handing her the proper item and its coupon, she will testily inform you that the coupon should be presented AFTER she totals your item. If, on the other hand, you had waited to present your coupon until after she had totalled your item, you would have been informed in the same testy tone of voice that "coupons have to be presented first." This is part of "the system," and only women know the precise moment that coupons should be tendered.

When you get home with your purchase, which of course is the wrong thing, your wife will sweetly ask what took you so long. DON'T FALL INTO THIS TRAP as she already knows what happened (the supermarket has probably called about you). By relating your tale of woe, you are only encouraging her to plot your next use of "the coupon" with added zeal. Tell her instead that you met an old high school girl friend and invited her out for a cup of coffee. That will keep her mind off coupons for awhile.

For the next two weeks while you are sleeping on the couch, vow never to use coupons again. The next time you "Go-to-the-store-for-your-wife," cheerfully take the coupon and then drive to the closest store, buy something similar to what she wants (it won't be the right thing anyway), and spend the time and money saved by browsing through your favorite sporting goods store or playing a round of golf. Just don't forget to swallow the coupon before you get home!

WOMEN'S PURSES

C ontributing to the rare and wonderful world of confusion surrounding man's understanding of women are the "tools of the trade" used by these marvelous creatures. Chief among this paraphernalia are the mysterious "women's purses"—curious containers of various sizes, owned, operated, and fiercely protected by females of all ages.

As befitting any good mystery, there are things about a woman's purse best left unknown to men. Without her purse, a woman is just a, well, a woman. With it, she becomes SUPERPERSON, a combination mother, doctor, handyman, movie star, and auto mechanic. Given the contents of a small purse, the average woman can overhaul an electronic typewriter, repair a car, diaper a baby, render medical assistance to a prize fighter, pick a lock, and perform minor surgery on a child's owie. This is in addition to the usual clothing and cosmetic stuff that women use to transform themselves into someone else.

Women's purses defy all known physical laws concerning volume and space. As a minimum, they usually contain candy bars, gum, keys to everything you ever wanted to open, a small knife, baby stuff, a handkerchief, wallet, checkbook, enough Kleenex (new and used) to wipe the noses of 35 kids, thirty paper clips, coins from at least two countries, Band-Aids, needle and thread, pins, a small screw driver, mouth freshener, three earrings, four little pieces of wadded-up paper, perfume, an out of date store coupon, breath mints, cosmetics, aspirin, at least one candy bar wrapper, a paperback novel, two broken key chains, Scotch Tape, and a few assorted postage stamps—and these are just the basics!

If you empty the average woman's purse on a rather large table, the contents would take up approximately seven cubic feet of space. Yet a woman, who never has enough closet space, can put all that stuff into a purse no larger than a doggie bag. This is one of the seven mysteries of the world and one of the things that men are simply not supposed to understand. You can, however, put your knowledge of women's purses to use: If, for example, you are ever stranded in the wilderness or find yourself in a survival situation, your best bet is to secure a woman's purse. With it you can eat, clothe yourself, handle emergency medical problems, defend yourself, fix your vehicle, and even buy your way out of trouble — all while having sweet breath.

WOMEN

I have never professed a keen insight into the workings of women's minds, but occasional inspired and lucid moments of understanding do happen. For instance, the shrieking, shouting, and waving of arms that occurs when my wife finds our offspring and me in the kitchen is merely her way of expressing unbridled joy and delight at the prospect of another father-son-daughter "bonding session." Most men in her situation would simply smile and walk away, savoring this moment of father/child closeness. But not women! The particular woman that I am married to usually trembles a lot, her shoulders slump, and she starts muttering about "hours of cleaning." Why someone would choose to think of cleaning the house in a tender moment like this is beyond me!

At this point I tend to believe this particular behavior pattern in American females is rather widespread, as most of my male friends report similar reactions from their wives when they and their kids head for the kitchen or announce that they are going to cook dinner. Shrieking, incomprehensible shouting, trembling and always the muttering about cleaning or housekeeping or some such nonsense occurs. Lacking other logical explanations, I think that it has something to do with hormones. The important thing here for men to understand is that this type of behavior on the part of women when they discover their husbands and children in their kitchens is probably normal and not to be feared. It is merely the female way of expressing joy and delight.

For a man to be reasonably successful at living in a house with women and children in it, he must make every effort at understanding females — that is, he must make allowances for them. Under no circumstances should the husband/father use logic when confronted with the female reaction to a given situation. For instance, last week I heard my wife shrieking in the kitchen. At first I just thought that she was very happy about something, but when I heard her muttering about husbands and children, I suspected something was wrong.

Note To Beginning Husbands/Fathers: *It is not a good sign when wives/mothers mutter under their breath about husbands/children. Caution is always called for because the husband/father and/or his child(ren) are usually in serious trouble for absolutely no reason at all. Don't try to figure it out as whole groups of men sitting in hunting camps and bars around the nation have devoted millions of man-hours to this same subject. The best they can come up with is that it has something to do with hormones.*

On entering the kitchen, I noticed my wife standing in battle formation, hands on hips, feet slightly apart, and my two little boys (ages 3 and 5) lined up in front of her in defensive formation (little one in front, big one behind). On closer inspection, I noticed that every flat surface in the entire kitchen, both vertical and horizontal, had been covered with paper towels and

Scotch Tape. The boys were going to make peanut butter and jelly sandwiches and thought the paper towels would make her clean-up job a lot easier.

When I expressed the opinion that it looked like a good idea to me and that the boys had shown both  brilliance and initiative, she gave me that icy, cold, slit-eyed stare that she usually reserves for rapists and child molesters. When I tried to explain to her that even NASA covers the space shuttle with tiles to prevent damage and that our kids were right up there with the nation's top engineers, she actually leered at me and, for a moment, I thought that she was going to bite. Sensing that the boys and I were in somewhat more doo-doo than usual, I snatched a calculator and showed her that the boys had only used 28 cents worth of towels and tape to protect a $12,000 kitchen. Very cost effective I thought and not entirely without merit.

About this time, her lips narrowed to a fine, thin, rather colorless line, and in a very curt, clipped voice stated that "that was not the issue." Then I made the mistake of innocently asking what the issue was. Later that night as the boys and I were having dinner at McDonalds's, I tried to explain to them that although their idea was logical and sound, their mom just didn't see it that way. When they asked why, about all I could come up with, based on my vast experience with women, was that it had something to do with hormones.

Part of the fascination of living with these wonderful and rather curious creatures is the tremendous difference between the sexes. I'm not referring to the obvious delightful differences but to the more subtle ones that tend to confound the male being on a daily basis. Why do women, for instance, button their shirts up the back where they can't possibly reach the buttons? Why do women have a closet full of clothes and yet have "nothing to wear"? Why do women grow older until they reach forty and then begin to grow younger? Why do women insist on wearing panty hose that "drive them crazy" or shoes that are uncomfortable and hurt their feet?

This is part of the female mystique. As a man/husband/father, you are supposed to understand these things and it is to your advantage to pretend to do so. DO NOT ask the obvious questions: "Well, if they hurt your feet, why do you wear them?" She'll just glare at you. If you push the issue too far, she'll say something like "I'm wearing them for you." Now, most men of my acquaintance harbor little or no desire to wear odd little shoes that hurt their feet, and the fact that women are willing to endure the pain and agony of wearing them "for us" adds to the confusion.

Somewhere along the line, probably eons ago, some neanderthal bought a pair of shoes that were too tight. Instead of throwing them away, his thrifty-minded wife decided to wear them. She soon became a martyr to the other cave women who quickly adapted the idea of painful feet as being "fashionable."

This tenet of womanhood has been handed down from woman to woman for centuries and by now is in their genes. They can't help it and you can't do anything about it. I suppose this is an admirable trait in women, but one that is misplaced. I don't buy shoes that are uncomfortable and hurt my feet, and if I did, I certainly wouldn't ask her to wear them for me. That women still go out and buy such shoes "for us" and then endure the pain of wearing them without being asked to, indicates that some members of this group may not be in complete control.

I once asked an otherwise intelligently dressed woman (my wife) why she buttoned her blouse up the back. She looked at me icily and her lips began to form a snarl, no doubt because I had dared to probe a level of female intellect heretofore unpenetrated by man. Quickly sensing danger and recognizing her look as one frequently given in response to my innocent questions, I immediately left the room and sought refuge amongst our children.

Note: *Women tend to avoid violence in front of children, therefore, a small child or two should be kept in the immediate vicinity if you anticipate asking anything other than where the car keys are.*

My kids, intuitive little brats, instantly chorused "What did you do now, Dad?" That's becoming a rather common question around our house.

Living with females can be frustrating and hazardous unless you learn how to handle the consequences of having them around on a daily basis. For example, women have a marvelous propensity for remembering trivial, unimportant things like names, birthdates, and eye color of third and fourth cousins, and on which side of the plate the forks go, but can't seem to remember to release the parking brake before driving the car. The fact that the vehicle seems sluggish, smells horrible, has the "parking brake" light illuminated on the dash, trails smoke, and decelerates quickly when she lets off the gas, does not invoke curiousity in the female mind, or, for that matter, even register. When she informs you that the "car smelled funny today," use your knowledge of women to insure your peaceful and harmonious co-existence by complimenting her on noticing the odor, and then quietly have the parking brake replaced.

It is a known fact that husbands cannot train wives effectively by speaking to them slowly and clearly. If you are looking for a high degree of retention, you must resort to artifice. In the case of parking brakes, pay some woman to start a rumor in the beauty salon that parking brakes should be released before driving cars and she'll come home gushing with the news. DO NOT say that you told her the same thing 37 times and DO NOT turn blue in the face. Instead, listen intently, and then wonder aloud why automobile manufacturers don't publish such information in the owner's handbook.

In the epic saga of men living with women, many pitfalls exist that require husbands/lovers to display great knowledge and skill in extracting themselves from the quicksand of female intrigue. Symbolic of the dangerous plots used by females to undermine domestic tranquility is one called **"The Trap."** Usually sprung on the male when he is in deep concentration (and the female is feeling lonely or neglected), she'll begin with something like "Honey, do you remember the little dress I was wearing when we first met?"

Right about now, the hairs on the back of your neck should be standing on end and your internal warning system blaring, because one wrong answer such as "uh huh" and she's got you! Obviously, the next question is "what color was it?" And of course, you don't remember. Had you answered "no" to the original question, she would have skipped the second, because the look of hurt on her face is actually a sign of victory and should be worth at least dinner out, or a new dress, depending on your current economic situation.

Women have at least a thousand versions of **"The Trap"** and always spring them when you least expect it. They are very good at this game and your only defense is to avoid a direct answer. Don't try to compete with her as this girl who can't remember to show up on time can remember trivia from your third date, your fourth date, and your second anniversary. You don't stand a chance!

A proper defense would be to stare into her eyes for a few moments (using this time to collect your wits), and say something like "The most memorable thing about that date were your eyes, they were the deepest, most striking blue that I had ever seen. (Or brown, green, etc., as appropriate. Don't make a mistake here.) I was swimming in them and nothing else in the whole world mattered." You have just won an instant tactical victory. To prevent her from regrouping and trying to salvage the situation, follow up with something like "and I'm still absolutely enchanted by your beauty — Say, would you mind getting me a cup of coffee?" When she brings the coffee, notice the sweet/sad smile on her face. Sweet because of the things that you said and sad because she lost the battle (and dinner out). You've not only gained a cup of coffee, but a brief respite from

entrapment while she tries to figure out what happened.

Certain characteristics of females cannot be circumvented and must simply be endured. Such is the case with women when it comes to food. Women can have some very unusual tastes, which should not be surprising since women can be very unusual creatures at times. Once my wife and I went to a nation-wide choke and puke for lunch. I ordered a reuben sandwich (sauerkraut, swiss cheese, and corned beef on rye) and received instead something that probably once resembled the venerable sandwich, but had now been rolled in powdered sugar! The thing was disgusting.

My wife's eyes, however, lit up and followed it across the table as I pushed it as far away from me as possible. Being of a scientific bent and curious as to whether human beings would actually eat such things, I naturally offered it to my wife. Now, I won't say that her actions were those of someone who had been deprived of food for several months, but they came pretty close. She devoured the concoction and proclaimed the revolting thing delicious. Of course I was stunned and asked her quite bluntly if she was pregnant. She said "of course not" and from the look on her face, I knew that it would be quite some time before I could justify asking her that question again.

Now some people may fault me for not even trying a bite of that "sandwich" before giving it a shove, but those folks are simply not using their God-given ability to discern good from bad. We should all realize that certain things just don't go together — oil and water, republicans and democrats, chocolate ice cream with spinach on top, obedience and children, and reuben sandwiches with powdered sugar.

Given his wife/girlfriend/sweetheart's penchant for odd tastes, the developing "Old Indian" cook should not be swayed by her occasional comments concerning his cooking. Women do things differently than men and the "Old Indian" method of cooking is about as different as you can get. This alone will bring on lots of head shaking, hand wringing and "tisk-tisking." The fact that you and your kids are producing edible food with your "unorthodox" methods will be a constant source of annoyance to her, which, in turn, should provide a constant source of amusement to you.

Basically, her mother taught her how things should be done in the kitchen. Over the years these things have become firmly entrenched and are now inviolate — dumb things like putting lids back on containers and wiping the goop off the counter before it becomes hard and has to be chiseled off. You'll just have to put up with these little idiosyncrasies if she's around. If not, feel free to do as you damn well please. At first she may say something about "cleaning up the mess being part of cooking" but we all know better. Cooking is cooking and cleaning up the mess is, well, cleaning up the mess — something to be avoided if possible. You may have to dodge a few slings and arrows about "slovenly ways," but your wife will eventually develop a damage control program that doesn't involve you and the kids.

Some less fortunate men have wives that actually INSIST that they clean up the kitchen after creating an "Old Indian" masterpiece. These are the same women who a) developed the habit of hanging around their own homes when they suspect father/child kitchen activity is afoot, or b) possess only a rudimentary amount of docility. In either case, there are several methods to get out of cleaning up the kitchen.

The one I favor most is called **"The Flood."** Here's how it works: When your wife appears on the verge of losing her civil demeanor, cheerfully volunteer to clean up the mess. In the process use lots of water — enough to fill your neighbor's pool is about right. Be sure to leave at least two inches on the floor. Next, slosh over to your wife, throw your arms around her and announce, "It's all cleaned up honey, spic and span." Note the look of horror on her face as she lunges for the mop and furiously begins transferring water from the floor to your once clean sink.

When they've got the floor reasonably dry, many women will then wax the whole area on their hands and knees. This is good as wives normally hate waxing floors more than they hate cleaning up after husbands. Usually this will get you out of future kitchen clean up immediately. However, I have heard of cases where several exposures to "the flood" were required before "Old Indian" cooks were banned by their wives from cleaning kitchens anymore. Persistence and determination are everything when dealing with women.

TRANSLATIONS

(Glossary of terms used by females and what they mean in English)

"ASK YOUR FATHER" — Term used by women when they want to pass the buck.

"DARLING, DO YOU REMEMBER THE SMITHS?" — They are either coming to your house for dinner or you are going to theirs. Usually stated when the female senses that you would like a quiet evening at home.

"THE CAR SMELLS FUNNY" — She left the emergency brake on.

"THE HOUSE IS FALLING DOWN AROUND OUR EARS" — You postponed a couple of "honey-do" jobs to watch the football game and then forgot all about them.

"HEAD OF HOUSEHOLD" — Term used by married women when they want the man to feel that he is the boss. Sometimes used when a salesman is at the door and they don't want to talk to him.

"ISN'T THAT CUTE?" — One of your smaller children is destroying something of yours.

"THAT KID IS A LITTLE MONSTER" — One of your smaller children is destroying something of HERS.

"DO YOU THINK I'M TOO _____?" (fill in the blank — fat, thin, over dressed, under dressed, tall, short, etc.) — Leading question. This means that at the moment she thinks that she is too _____. DO NOT agree with her. Always answer in the negative, "No, dear, you are not too fat (tall, skinny, etc.). You're just right," regardless of what you really think. Remember that old saying "A man who will not lie to his wife has no consideration for her feelings." Wives want compliments, not truth.

"DO I LOOK OK?" — She is searching for a compliment from you after three hours of preparation to look great for other people. See above.

"OH, YOU'RE JUST BEING SILLY" — Used in front of the kids when you state that liver tastes terrible or that you see no redeeming social value in opera.

"YOUR" SON or "YOUR" CHILDREN — Your children are in serious trouble, and, since they are "yours," you are responsible, and therefore, in trouble too.

"NOTHING TO WEAR" — Her closet is bulging with clothing that she doesn't want to wear right now (but will not throw away). Plead poverty or tell her the truth — that you are saving every penny for her new outboard motor.

"NOTHING" — Usually an answer given to the question "what's the matter, honey?" When this occurs, you are in SERIOUS trouble with her. You have probably forgotten her birthday, the fourteenth anniversary of your first date, not noticed her new hairdo/dress, or that she lost 2 lbs. It could also mean that she caught you eyeballing the neighbor in her new bikini. This word has the potential of being very expensive.

"WHAT DO YOU THINK, DEAR?" — Direct order to agree with her or admire what she is wearing. Do not assume that your honest opinion is actually being sought.

"YOUR CHILDREN WERE IMPOSSIBLE TODAY" — The children were normal kids. SHE had a bad day. Watch out!

"MEN!" — Usually accompanied by eyes rolled toward the sky. A form of showing exasperation or annoyance with something you did (like washing the kids with the garden hose).

"WHAT WOULD YOU LIKE FOR DINNER, DEAR?" — She is either out of ideas for what to fix for dinner, or missing some of the ingredients for what she would like to fix. Do not assume that she's actually interested in taking your order like a waitress. She already knows what you like and would fix it if so inclined, which she's not.

"YOU'RE THE BOSS DEAR" — means she will follow your dictates insofar as they are not inconsistent with her own desires — Or she is doubtful about the outcome and wants you to shoulder the blame.

"OH, JUST ANYWHERE" — Answer given in response to question "where would you like to go to eat, honey?" Female has definite idea of where she would like to go, but you are supposed to guess. If you guess wrong, she will spend the entire evening talking about how much better the food/atmosphere/service is at the place you didn't guess. Women are particularly fond of this game and play it often. The national average for correct guessing is less than 1%.

SECTION TWO

"Old Indian" Recipes

T he recipes in this cookbook are designed to be fun, easy to make, use as few utensils as possible, and taste good. They are perfect for father/child creative kitchen projects regardless of the age of either. Kids tend to become a little older and fathers a little younger when using this book and "playing" together in the kitchen.

DEFINITIONS

TEASPOON — If you are allowed to use your wife's gadgets, she has a neat little metal or plastic spoon-like thing with a small handle. Somewhere on it should be the letters "tsp." That's a teaspoon. If you are not allowed to use her stuff, use the first smallish spoon that you come to in the drawer. That's close enough. Lacking this, four good sized pinches between the side of your forefinger and thumb is about one teaspoon of whatever you are measuring. This requires a little dexterity with liquids.

TABLESPOON — Similar to wife's gadget above but with "tbsp." on the handle. Equivalent to three teaspoons, twelve pinches, or the large size spoon in the drawer.

CAN — Don't worry about exact can sizes or numbers. When I say "can" I mean your average sized can — a little more or less is OK. If I specify a big can, I mean just that — a great huge can. An itty-bitty can is about the size of the ones that they put the little pieces of dead tuna in. A "can" holds about twice as much as an itty-bitty can and about half as much as a big can.

DASH — I have no idea, so you won't find it used in this book.

A LITTLE — Whatever amount seems right at the moment.

A LOT — More than "a little."

CUP — Glass, metal or plastic container with math symbols on it. Your wife probably has one of these things hidden in plain sight (women do that a lot) but don't waste time looking for it — just grab a cup. Any cup. A cup's a cup.

FRYING PAN — Big round metal or glass thing with low sides and a long handle. Probably has warped bottom.

SAUCE PAN — Smaller round metal or glass thing with higher sides. Handle is optional.

SMOKE IN KITCHEN — Food possibly overdone.

BUTTER — Margarine of the solid type — usually in stick form, NOT the easy to spread stuff in the little plastic tub.

OIL — Cooking oil. Stay out of the garage or shop. This stuff is found somewhere in the kitchen and is made from vegetables, although I don't think they make it from normal vegetables. Oil made from peanuts, corn, criscos, olives, wessons or sunflowers is OK.

GROUND BEEF — This does not mean ground chuck or ground round. It's the cheapest kind of ground-up cow.

FLOUR — Fine white powder-like stuff that comes in a bag labeled "flour." Women usually take it out of the bag and put it in another container (usually with little flowers on it or the word "flour") and imbed some form of scoop in it. There are several types of flour such as "all purpose," "self rising," "pastry," etc. Don't worry about this, just use whatever your wife has on hand. A word of caution here — don't use the stuff in the little boxes labeled "Bisquick" or "pancake flour" unless directed to do so.

PAPER PLATES — God's gift to the world's fathers. They're cheap, they work, kids love them, and they don't have to be washed. Use two per kid, one on top of the other.

TEMPERATURE SETTINGS (STOVE, OVEN) — Some stove controls have settings on them such as low, medium, and high, while others offer a bunch of little dots and infinite settings. Still others offer actual degrees of temperature. Don't let any of this intimidate you.

OVERDONE — Yucky black color — hard on bottom, sides, and top. May be accompanied by smoke in kitchen. Neighbor's dog will not eat.

UNDERDONE — Characterized by lack of smoke in kitchen. This phenomenon should put the "Old Indian" cook on alert that underdone condition may exist. Primary ingredients, such as potatoes, carrots, celery, etc., are hard and loosely resemble those found in a salad bar. Breads, biscuits, pancakes, will be gooey and messy.

STUFF — Generally refers to ingredients.

VEGETABLES

Most fathers will try to avoid the area of parental brutality known as "Forcing your kids to eat their vegetables." This is an area best left to the kids' mother as YOU don't want to be associated with these early childhood emotional scars. There are basically two ways around this situation. First, recognize that children don't like "yucky stuff" any more than you do. My 2½ year old daughter, "Ralph," will eat paper, bugs, dirt, and an occasional plastic toy, but not brussels sprouts. A sensible child. Likewise, my five year old son "Bumper" will not touch yucky creamed cauliflower but will eat wholesome, healthy stuff like corn-on-the-cob and peas.

The problem is that some yo-yo convinced the majority of American women in high school home economics class that a healthy, balanced diet included vegetables — all kinds of vegetables. Your best bet is to get your kids to like the same kinds of vegetables that you like. This way, the only person in the house who will eat the truly yucky stuff like brussels sprouts, broccoli, or carrots, is your wife. Since this will make her appear "odd," or at least unusual, to the rest of the family (and no woman wants to appear odd), she will refrain from serving such horrible stuff on a regular basis.

On those rare occasions when she slips some stewed tomatoes on the menu, she can't very well force the entire family to gag them down. Since she's the only one who will eat them, she'll be eating them for a week (women don't throw "good food" away). By the end of this time, the stewed tomatoes will have lost a lot of their appeal to her and it will be a long time before you see them again.

In spite of the nasty looks you will get from your wife, you can assist in this process by making faces at the stewed tomatoes (or other dreadful vegetables), uttering obnoxious gagging sounds and clutching at your throat. Kids are pretty smart and soon learn that stewed tomatoes (and other yucky vegetables) are not fit for human consumption. By assisting your children's education in this manner, you also help insure that more desirable vegetables, such as those YOU like, or tolerate reasonably well, are served to your family. This system works exceptionally well when used in front of guests.

The second method of avoiding the father/child/vegetable debacle lies in your own cooking. NEVER cook vegetables that you don't like. If a recipe calls for some particularly despicable vegetable, simply substitute something else. For instance, in the case of cauliflower in cheese sauce, substitute air for the cauliflower. If this doesn't have enough body for you, try green beans or asparagus.

Not all yucky vegetables (determined by the reader) should be spurned or avoided. In order to appear broad minded, I have included several recipes whereby certain yucky vegetables (such as carrots) can actually be decontaminated and made edible.

Note: *By now, the reader may have come to the conclusion that I harbor a special hatred for stewed tomatoes. Actually this is not true as I hate ALL forms of tomato where the tomato can still be identified as a tomato. Catsup, ketchup, and tomato sauce are OK. Basically, I regard tomatoes as an obnoxious substance put on my plate solely to trigger my gag reflex.*

Carrots and cauliflower are not very high on my list either. If you like these vegetables, consume all you like, but I will not assist you in this form of self destruction.

A little known fact (concealed by the tomato, carrot, and cauliflower companies) is that 97% of all pilots involved in fatal airplane crashes have eaten either tomatoes, cauliflower, or carrots (or worse — all three) sometime during the 60 days preceeding their last flight. The insidious tentacles of these vegetable companies reach the highest levels of the National Transportation Safety Board where a major cover-up has managed to hide the fact that 99% of all drivers involved in automobile accidents come from families where tomatoes, cauliflower, and carrots were served regularly! What's more, I suspect that a large portion of our criminal population consumes these vegetables on an almost daily basis!

The eating of these obnoxious vegetables is a learned trait. Mothers stuff strained carrots and cauliflower into the mouths of innocent, helpless babies from the time they are able to spit it out until they are old enough to eat on their own. And still it goes on, just bigger pieces and larger portions.

Nature trys to assist young children by making these vegetables taste bad, but by the time kids become young adults, many actually LIKE the taste. Ask any child who has not yet reached this terminal  stage whether he or she prefers a stewed tomato over a hot fudge sundae, or a dish of creamed carrots over a chocolate caramel candy bar, or a large helping of steamed cauliflower over a root beer float and the vegetables will lose every time (unless the kid is already ruined).

There are plenty of decent vegetables out there for us to eat without asking for trouble. This cookbook provides several methods of preparing and using alternative vegetables. The time has come to eradicate stuff like creamed carrots, stewed tomatoes and steamed cauliflower from the American diet!

BROCCOLI WITH CHEESE SAUCE

(Beginner's gourmet cooking from a can)

It is a well known fact that children and most big people will not eat broccoli if given an alternative (no TV, banishment, or death by tickling). However, this particularly obnoxious vegetable can be made edible by the magic of simple "saucery."

Some fresh broccoli
or
Some frozen whole broccoli spears
1 can Campbell's cheese soup
Some tarragon

Fresh broccoli — If you (and not your wife) buy this stuff, look for tightly closed dark green flowerets and firm but tender stalks. Wash thoroughly and remove the large outer leaves. Cut off any of the stalk that appears tough. The stalks take longer to cook than the "flowerets" so you can do several things with them: a) cut the stalks off and partially cook them before adding the flowerets, b) leave the stalks attached but split them into quarters (slice from bottom almost up to the floweret), or c) stand the spears upright in the pan and add water to cover the stalk. This will boil the tougher parts and steam the more tender flowerets. Whichever way you chose, cook the stuff in a covered pan in boiling water and a little tarragon for about 12 to 15 minutes total or until tender. Drain thoroughly.*

Frozen broccoli — follow the directions on the package but add a little tarragon to the water, about a half teaspoon, no more. Drain thoroughly.*

Open the can of Campbell's cheese soup and heat according to the instructions on the can. Do not add water. Now completely destroy the can as you are going to pretend that you made the cheese sauce yourself. This is completely acceptable as gourmet cooking is a devious business anyway. Pour the bubbling cheese sauce over the cooked broccoli (assuming that the broccoli has been placed on a serving dish) and serve immediately. People will rave about your broccoli and ask you for the recipe. Don't give it to them. Instead, give them the name of your cookbook and where you bought it.

*Drain thoroughly. *This is very important. Get all the water off the broccoli or it will dilute your cheese sauce and make the whole thing a watery mess. Your wife probably has a bowl-shaped thing with a bunch of holes in the bottom called a "colander." This does a pretty good job of draining things but for best results use a towel. Just dump the vegetable in a towel and twist it up so that nothing can fall out. Now go outside and sling the towel around your head a few times. The vegetable will be bone dry, which is what we want. Your wife may frown on this practice, so use the colander if you spot her lurking around, otherwise use the towel. If she calls your attention to the green stains on the towel at some later date, mutter something about "mold" and then quickly go outside and work on the car.*

Comment on "Campbell's" — *Once or twice in our lifetime a company will come along that truly benefits mankind. Such a company is Campbell Soup Company. They make really excellent stuff that not only tastes good, but that can cut your kitchen work load by about two thirds. Just try making a good cheese sauce that doesn't curdle or separate, and you will find yourself slaving over a hot stove for longer than you care to think about. As an "Old Indian" cook, you are concerned with results and not the hours that you spend in the kitchen. There is nothing wrong with using products that save both time and money and we will use these products throughout this book. Just price a nice hunk of cheese in the supermarket and you'll understand. By the way, I don't own any stock in Campbell's but I'd sure like to.*

BUTTER CARROTS

(The only known method for making carrots palatable)

**1 can carrots sliced or whole
or
6 or 7 raw carrots
¼ cup butter (half a "stick")
"Touch" of nutmeg**

Empty the can of carrots into a large sauce pan and drain off the liquid. Add enough water to cover the carrots and bring to a boil. Simmer for 2 or 3 minutes (turn heat down to "low" or last dot on knob). Drain off water.

or

If using whole, fresh carrots, clean the outside of each by thoroughly washing or scraping with a knife or potato peeler. Cut off the top and bottom half inch and cut lengthwise into quarters. Now boil the carrots in water until they become reasonably soft. Drain and replace the water (about two cups), bring to a boil again and reduce heat to "simmer" for 2 or 3 minutes. Drain off water.

With either canned or fresh carrots you are now ready to proceed by placing the carrots in the bowl or dish that you intend to serve them in (saves washing another bowl). Dump ALL the butter and the touch of nutmeg in the original sauce pan. Heat over medium heat (halfway on the dial, dummy) until the butter begins to bubble. Now throw the carrots in and INCREASE the heat to medium high. Stir frequently and gently (so as not to break the carrots into little pieces) until they just begin to brown on the edges.

Quickly remove from heat, drain off the excess butter, add a sprig or two of parsley for eye appeal and serve. I have never met a human being that didn't like these carrots, even a notorious carrot hater like me. For some reason this process gets rid of the bitter carrot taste and makes even old carrots taste sweet. Try it.

FANCY
GREEN BEANS

I stole this recipe from a friend of mine who fancies himself as a pretty good cook, which he is. He's not very bright though, as I made these beans as part of a dinner we had for him and his wife and he asked me for the recipe! The only reason that I include it here is that nobody eats plain old green beans anymore. Apparently, the current fad is to "do something" to the beans or risk being socially ostracized. There must be a million people out there who are sick and tired of green beans swimming in cream of mushroom soup with crumbly things on top. Like all "Old Indian" recipes, this one is simple, quick, and tastes very good. Most people have recipes similar to this but they've been lost in the mushroom soup craze. It's up to you to resurrect this old-timer.

> **1 can French cut green beans**
> **2 or 3 tbsp. slivered almonds**
> **3 tbsp. butter**
> **1½ tsp. lemon juice**

Heat the beans according to the directions on the can. Drain thoroughly and place in serving dish. In the same pan, cook the almonds in butter over LOW heat until they're a golden color, stirring frequently. Remove pan from heat and add the lemon juice. Now pour over the hot green beans, toss lightly and serve. You can vary this recipe by substituting a couple of strips of chopped up bacon for the slivered almonds and using the bacon drippings instead of the butter.

Note: *Don't try to sliver the almonds yourself or you'll wind up slivering your fingers instead. You BUY slivered almonds already slivered in tiny little packages with large price tags.*

SPINACH SOUFFLE

Actually, this recipe has little to do with real souffles, which are a pain in the butt to make. Besides, men don't eat souffles. This is a good way to get your kids to eat spinach as it doesn't taste yucky.

2 cans spinach
4 beaten egg whites* or 3 whole eggs
½ tsp. nutmeg
Some salt and pepper
Butter

Preheat oven to 350 degrees (the Old Indian cook ALWAYS preheats his oven). Open the cans of spinach but leave the lids loosely on top. Now go to the sink and drain the liquid by inverting the can and shoving the lid up into the spinach, squashing the contents but forcing most of the liquid out. Remove the lids and dump the spinach into a LARGE bowl to finish draining. When a little ring of greenish colored water forms around the spinach, drain it off. It's almost impossible to thoroughly drain canned spinach, but this will have to do.

If your wife is not at home or you are allowed to use her stuff, get her mixer out and insert the beaters. If not, get your electric drill and a piece of coat hanger about a foot long. Bend the hanger in an "L" shape so that the bottom of the "L" is about an inch and a half long. Chuck it in the drill. With either of these tools, proceed to chop the hell out of the spinach until it is nothing more than an amorphous mass. During this process, note that the spinach splatters all over the sides of the bowl. That's why I had you use a LARGE bowl, to keep it off the kitchen walls.

Add the eggs, nutmeg and salt and pepper and mix it in. Select a quart and a half size baking dish or one that will hold the goop at about the two inch level with a little room for expansion. Have the kid(s) grease the bowl with the butter and then add the spinach mixture. Pop it in the preheated oven for about forty minutes or until the center appears done. When you serve this dish, you MUST place a small pat of butter on top of each serving. It's delicious!

Egg whites are obtained by separating them from the egg yolk (very difficult task). Throw away the yolk unless a) your wife is watching or b) your wife is watching. If either a) or b) occurs, put the egg yolks in a small cup covered with plastic wrap and place in the refrigerator for later disposal. Women always put egg yolks in a small cup covered with plastic wrap in the refrigerator until a film forms on the yolk. At that time the yolks are thrown away. Apparently women suspect that garbage men will reject their garbage if they find an egg yolk in it without a film on it. Rumors abound that a woman in Alabama actually USES the egg yolks in her refrigerator in the cup with plastic wrap on it for cooking.

Rumors being what they are, and having lived with women most of my life, I tend to pass this one off as poppycock. Just throw the yolk away.

THE "WHAT THE HELL DO YOU DO WITH ZUCCHINI" RECIPE

In my part of the country EVERYBODY grows zucchini because everybody CAN grow zucchini. There is nobody on the face of the earth that cannot successfully grow tons of zucchini. One zucchini plant will produce 47,000 zucchinis. The local sport is to see who can give the most zucchini away before they get shot. We usually board up our windows and doors, turn the lights out early, and let the newspapers stack up on the front lawn during "zucchini season."

Nevertheless, we usually wind up with several hundred of the things on hand (usually thrown over the back fence or mailed to us in packages marked, "You have just won _____ .") Since the garbage disposal will only handle so many zucchinis in a twenty-four hour period, and the city does not own enough garbage trucks to handle the annual crop, people wind up eating dozens of them. Obviously, some pretty creative cooking goes on.

After a while, people go around asking each other, "What the hell do you do with zucchini?" That's where this recipe comes in. EVERYBODY LOVES IT. You will be a hero in your own time, especially if you live in a "zucchini area".

Two large zucchinis, peeled
1 cup dry bread or cracker crumbs
½ cup grated parmesan cheese
½ cup flour
3 tsp. salt
Two eggs, beaten
Enough oil to cover bottom of pan ⅛ inch deep

In a plastic bag or on a large plate, combine the bread crumbs, cheese, flour, and salt. Slice the peeled zucchini fairly thin and dip in eggs (this is a little easier if you add two tsp. of water to the eggs before you beat them. Seems to stick better). Now coat the zucchini with crumb mixture and fry in hot oil until golden brown and crisp, turning once. Drain on paper towels and serve immediately.

Note: *Two zucchinis may sound like a lot of zucchini, but once people taste this stuff, it may not be enough. Doesn't taste anything like zucchini. Excellent at parties with various dips.*

WORLD'S BEST ONION RINGS

This recipe will make you a giant among those who like onion rings and an apostle of epicurean delight to those who once thought they didn't like them. Although this recipe has been in my "Old Indian" stable for years and has appeared in other cookbooks, I've never met a single person who has even heard of it, let alone tried it. In keeping with the underlying philosophy of "Old Indian" cooking, it is simple to the point of being ridiculous, tastes extremely good, and fools people into thinking that you know what you're doing after all.

Large onions
Buttermilk pancake mix
Peanut oil

Prepare rings out of the onions. Make sure that the onions are large (they're usually sweeter) and don't cut the slices from which you make the rings too thick. Mix up a bowl of the buttermilk pancake batter EXACTLY as the directions on the box tell you to. Dip the onion rings in the batter and fry in about ½ inch of HOT oil until golden brown. Drain on paper towels. Serve immediately and prepare yourself for a standing ovation. It is not uncommon for true onion ring gourmets to stand and bow at this point in recognition of your culinary genius.

Note on temperature and utensils: *By "hot," I don't mean for you to crank up the heat until the oil smokes. About 375 degrees or medium high should do it. Any pan will do but the heavier the better as this helps keep the oil temperature fairly constant. You can use a deep fat fryer but it takes longer to heat up and won't hold as many onion rings as a large skillet.*

PHONY BAKED BEANS

    "Real" baked beans require a lot of time and effort, which, of course, is against the basic principles of "Old Indian" cookery. One who wishes to slave over a hot stove for seven or eight hours to produce an edible product is, in my opinion, suffering from massive fundamental character flaws. The fact that phony baked beans taste just as good as "real" baked beans should provide you with a tremendous opportunity to lie about the hours you spent in the kitchen preparing this delightful treat for your family. In fact, these beans taste so much like the "real" thing that criminals have been known to use this recipe to establish an alibi for their whereabouts during the commission of a crime. Nobody can believe they didn't require hours and hours of attention and slow cooking.

3 16 oz. cans of cooked navy or great northern beans
⅔ cup brown sugar
1 tsp. dry mustard
¼ cup molasses
1 medium onion, diced
6 strips bacon

    Cook the bacon until crisp and place on paper towels. Cook the diced or chopped onion in the bacon fat until tender and slightly yellow. In a 2½ quart casserole dish or equal size pan, dump in the beans, drained onions, crumbled bacon, and all the rest of the stuff. Mix well and bake uncovered at 325 degrees for 1½ to 1¾ hours. Serves eight normal people, four very hungry people, or two teenagers.

    Note: *If you prefer New England style beans, cut the brown sugar in half and double the amount of* *molasses. I suggest that you taste the beans several times throughout the cooking cycle and adjust the amount of molasses and/or sugar according to your tastes. Add water if necessary.*

General Note on Vegetables

A lot of things can be done with plain old vegetables just as they come from the can or package to make then taste better and look more appealing. No serious cooking is required. Remember that half the appeal of food is EYE appeal. Make 'em look good and they seem to TASTE good. You can add a "topper" to almost any plain vegetable and people will think that it's something special. Use contrasting colors where possible. Try crumbled bacon, grated cheese, sliced or diced black olives, pimientos, or slices of hard boiled eggs. Use your imagination and try Philadelphia cream cheese or sour cream. And don't forget various nuts, mushrooms, or croutons (pieces of toast chopped up into little squares). People will think that you are a culinary genius, which you are because you are reading this book.

Cooking vegetables or making vegetable dishes is a wonderful way to start kids towards knowledge and independence in the kitchen. Most youngsters are completely helpless when it comes to cooking for themselves. Unless it's "instant," or only requires heating in a microwave oven, it's a foreign commodity to today's youth.

"Cooking with dad" is a neat way to spend some time together and maybe broaden a few horizons. Even very young kids can be part of the picture by helping dad in the kitchen. They can empty cans into bowls, wash the veggies, stir cold food, add seasonings, and a host of other things that make them feel like they are part of the action. They'll be as proud as punch. Just use your head to keep the little guys and gals safe—no sharp knives, no handles jutting out from the stove, no hot stuff around the kids, etc.

Remember that little people are absolutely magic! These little bundles of wonder can confuse you, impress you, baffle you, amaze you, stump you, warm your heart, refresh your soul, and always they love you. So take care of them in the kitchen just like you do elsewhere.

YUCKY LIVER THAT'S NOT YUCKY

Little kids are pretty smart. They won't eat broccoli and they won't touch liver. Can't say that I blame them. You can smother the stuff in onions, put tomatoes on it, or chop it up into pate, but as far as I'm concerned, it's still liver and it's still yucky. People who serve liver to other people should be shot—unless, of course, they use this recipe. It's the only known way to make the stuff socially acceptable. Until science finds a way to make cows without livers or women stop buying it (men don't buy liver), this recipe is our only hope. It's the minimum sort of thing that one can do to liver and still eat it. (It actually tastes pretty good.)

Some tender calves' liver (don't overdo it)
Ground sage
Garlic powder
Salt and pepper

First remove any veins or membranes from the liver (about ½ inch thick). Cut little slits all over it— both sides. Now rub salt and pepper, garlic powder, and LOTS of ground sage into the slits. Broil on both sides until done. This doesn't take very long, about 2 or 3 minutes per side. Do not overcook. Use a little applied psychology when putting it on the dinner table by not serving anything good with it. This way, the liver will seem even better than it is. Even kids will eat it IF you don't tell them beforehand that it's liver.

Note: *"Old Indian" cooks NEVER voluntarily cook liver. This is a self defense measure to be used ONLY if you discover that your wife has determined that sufficient time has lapsed since she last subjected the family to liver. Suspect foul play is afoot if she brings home a package wrapped in plain white paper from the supermarket and hides it in the back of the meat keeper. If you ask her "what's for dinner tonight?" and get an evasive answer, it's time to have the kids distract her while you pry open the package.*

Should it indeed prove to be this foul substance, quickly volunteer to cook supper and USE THIS RECIPE! It's your only salvation. I don't know why women do this, but a friend once suggested that it is a subconscious way of getting even with men and children for the pain of childbirth. Could be.

MEAT LOAF

I include this recipe only to assist you in establishing your reputation as one who can elevate ordinary food to a level of greatness normally reserved for more exotic fare. Aren't you glad somebody gave you this book?

1½ lbs. ground round
1 pkg. au jus mix
¼ cup chopped onions
¼ cup chopped green pepper
1 beaten egg
¼ cup milk
Salt and pepper
1 pkg. brown gravy mix

Note: This is the only place in this cookbook that you will use ground round instead of plain old hamburger. Refer to "Definitions" section.

Put the meat and half the package of au jus in a large bowl. Cook the onion and green pepper in a couple of tablespoons of butter until the onion turns yellow. Add this and the rest of the stuff to the ground round, reserving the remaining half of the au jus mix for the gravy. Thoroughly squish everything together and dump in a 9 x 6 loaf pan.

Place the pan in a preheated 375 degree oven for about an hour. During the last 15 minutes of cooking, make the brown gravy in the same pan that you cooked the onions in. Follow the package instructions. Now add the remaining au jus mix to the gravy. If you like mushrooms, add half an itty-bitty can to the gravy. Don't use fresh mushrooms here as they won't have time to cook. Serve the meat loaf with "Butter Carrots" and buttered new potatoes sprinkled with parsley.

You will receive a lot of compliments on this dish as it tastes more like roast beef than meat loaf. When asked about the seasonings you used, lie. Explain that there is no modern-day equivalent to the originals and that you had to traipse about in the wilderness for days to secure an adequate supply for this one meal. Everyone will believe you.

SALISBURY STEAK

One of the reasons that people don't have salisbury steak at home anymore (unless it's in a TV dinner) is that it takes too long to fix. This is nonsense, as this recipe will take less than 10 minutes of your time to make (exclusive of cooking time). Some people claim that the Earl of Salisbury invented this meal, but that's also nonsense as they didn't have grinded-up cow in the 16th century. It wasn't until Bubba Crammer's milk cow got caught in the cotton gin that grinded-up cow became the staple of poor people. If you are a yuppie, don't eat this stuff.

> 1½ lbs. ground beef
> 1 can Campbell's Golden Mushroom Soup
> 1 small onion, chopped
> 2 eggs, beaten
> Salt and pepper
> ¼ cup milk
> ¼ tsp. cinnamon

In a large bowl, mix all the ingredients except ⅔ of the Golden Mushroom Soup. Shape into 5 or 6 patties and arrange in a single layer in an 8 by 12 inch baking dish. Place uncovered in a preheated 350 degree oven for about 30 minutes. Drain off the grease. Mix the remaining soup with ¼ cup water and pour over the meat. Bake for fifteen more minutes at 300 degrees. Top with chives or chopped green onions. Serve with mashed potatoes and fancy green beans.

"BLUE PLATE SPECIAL"

Remember the old days when every mom and pop restaurant had a "blue plate special" for a buck or two? It was nothing more than a plate-full of good tasting, home style food without the frills. They made the stuff in large batches and served a lot of it. Some say the name "blue plate" came from the color of the plate that it was served on. Others say it got its name from the mostly "blue collar" workers that bought the stuff. Either way, it wouldn't make it in a dainty French restaurant. Neither would the clientele who ate it. The mom and pop patron wanted solid food that "filled the hole" for a reasonable price.

One of the best such meals that I've ever eaten was served in a little cafe in a logging town named Libby, in northwest Montana. If memory serves correctly, I paid $1.49 for the "special" and all the coffee I could drink (and it wasn't that many years ago!). This recipe is an attempt to duplicate that meal. It should be served with gobs of mashed potatoes smothered with gravy, buttered peas, and hot biscuits.. If you don't have any blue colored plates, that's OK. A spray can of blue enamel and a few of your wife's everyday plates will do nicely. Just tell her that you are taking a trip down memory lane. She'll understand.

1 lb. ground beef
1 itty-bitty can sliced mushrooms
Some bread crumbs
½ cup diced onions
2 beaten eggs
Salt and pepper
Touch of nutmeg

In a large bowl, mix the ground beef, onions, one egg, salt and pepper, and just a shake or two of nutmeg. Now divide the resulting mess into two lumps. On a cutting board or other flat surface, form four oval-shaped patties out of one lump. Cover the top of each patty with sliced mushrooms. Now make four identical size patties from the other lump and cover the "mushroomed" patties with these. Pinch the edges together. Coat each with egg first and then bread crumbs.

This is rather difficult as the patties are kind of wimpy and you'll probably break them in the process. Your best bet is to smear a little egg on top of each, spread some bread crumbs around on top of that and then turn the patties over and repeat the process. Use a large spatula or your kid's garden shovel to turn them over without breaking. The same tool puts them in the frying pan (one ingenious acquaintance even uses a metal dust pan, scrubbed, of course. Don't let your wife catch you doing this.)

In about ⅛ inch of oil, cook for 5 to 10 minutes on each side over medium heat. Serve with gravy made from one package brown gravy mix and ½ package au jus mix. To this gravy, add one can Campbell's Golden Mushroom soup, full strength. Stir well. Spoon over meat patty and potatoes. Serve plates with food already on them. Don't forget the biscuits!

LITTLE PEOPLE PIZZA

I freely admit stealing this idea from the side of an
English muffin package. Once these people's
advertising departments entice me to buy a product
with a neat sounding recipe, that recipe becomes mine.
If some muffin company out there is upset that I'm
passing their concoction along in this book, I apologize
and hereby give them credit for the recipe. I just
wonder if they did the same thing to whoever THEY
stole it from. Remember, there is no such thing as an
original recipe.

1 pkg. plain English muffins
1 8 oz. can tomato sauce
Mozzarella or Monterey Jack cheese
Meat (sausage, pork, hamburger, etc.)
Italian or pizza seasoning (or use oregano w/touch
ground sage)

Split the English muffins in half and lightly toast
them. (If you don't they'll be mushy.) While this is
going on, cook the sausage, hamburger, pork, etc. and
drain on paper towels. Now spread a layer of tomato
sauce on the muffin halves and sprinkle with
seasoning. Don't use too much as the tomato sauce is
already seasoned. Give it a taste test first. If you don't
have pizza or Italian seasoning, try the oregano and
add just a hint of ground sage. Most people actually
like this combo better than the one with the "factory"
seasonings, but suit yourself.

Put some grated or thin sliced cheese on next and
then add whatever topping that your taste buds

suggest. Experiment all you like. Don't forget the veggies—mushrooms, green pepper, onions, olives, etc. If you don't like it, all you've ruined is half an English muffin and not a whole pizza. These little pizzas also allow you to individualize them for all your "customers". BE SURE that you precook all of the uncooked meat toppings as actual pizza cooking time is too short to do a thorough job on them.

Now place the little buggers on a baking sheet and pop in a preheated 325 degree oven until the cheese melts. This should only take a few minutes, so keep a close eye on what they're doing in the oven. Once you get the hang of making these little things, you can do the whole job, from start to finish, in less than 15 minutes. They go so great at parties that you may be asked to cater a few neighborhood affairs. Accept all offers and mail 50% of the take to me.

STOMACH ACHE STEW

Everyone has a recipe for stew, so I had originally intended not to include mine. However, my kids prevailed upon me to enrich the less fortunate by sharing this "Old Indian" delight. I think my kids like it because it covers up the repulsive taste of the vegetables. Like the rest of the recipes in this book, it is simple and delicious.

1 lb. beef stew meat
4 medium potatoes, peeled and cut into bite-sized pieces
4 medium carrots, peeled and cut into pieces
1 large onion, peeled and quartered
Some flour
Some garlic powder
1 pkg. au jus mix
2 pkgs. brown gravy mix
Salt and pepper

Put the flour in a large plastic bag and add about ¼ of the stew meat and shake, coating the meat thoroughly. Repeat this process until all the meat is floured. In a large pot, melt 3 or 4 tablespoons of butter and saute the floured chunks and quartered onion until the meat is nice and brown. Add enough water to cover and simmer for about 1½ hours. Make sure at least 2 or 3 cups of water are in the pan.

Now add the rest of the vegetables and seasonings to the pot and simmer for another 30 to 45 minutes or until meat and vegetables are tender. Remove everything from the pan except the liquid. Add the packages of au jus and brown gravy mix and beat it up with a mixer until smooth. Let cook for 10 minutes. If weak and thin, add a tablespoon of cornstarch dissolved in a little water and stir it in. Repeat if necessary. Now add the stuff that you took out earlier and gently mix it in. Let simmer for a few minutes and then serve with thick slices of hot French bread. You can't go wrong.

SLUM GULLIUM

(Old Indian word meaning "stuff")

This is one of those recipes that everyone has. You can throw it together in a matter of minutes, it always tastes the same, and everybody likes it. Similar food in the Army is called SOS and in the Marines #@%$&*#. In the Air Force it's called "Not this stuff again." These names, of course, are no reflection on the food. Military people just like to name things.

1½ lbs. of ground beef
2 cans Campbells' cream of mushroom soup
1 medium onion
Garlic powder

Chop or dice the onions and then brown them and the hamburger over medium heat in a large frying pan. When thoroughly browned, drain the grease and add the mushroom soup. Stir continuously while adding about a half cup of water. Add a little garlic powder and continue to stir until it just begins to bubble. Reduce heat to low and simmer for 5 minutes. Serve over hot buttered toast, mashed potatoes, or rice. Add carrots, celery, potatoes, peas, etc., and you have a passable mulligan. The stuff is pretty hard to mess up no matter what you add to it, so have at it. I use the basic recipe and just add mushrooms. Delicious! My kids even like it for breakfast.

YUPPIE SOUP

(Flavor treat known only to experimenters)

All this requires is the mixing together of several types of canned or packaged soup. This is not the cop-out that you think it is. The kids and I have a lot of fun with this stuff. My eight year old daughter "Button" suggested that we mix Campbell's chicken vegetable with cream of chicken and you can't believe the results. Tastes like the creamy soups served in restaurants, only better. When you serve this to your wife and/or guests, casually mention that it contains a blend of imported seasonings that you found in a tiny little gourmet shop. They'll go nuts trying to figure it out. Let them.

Just remember when you start combining soups that the cream soups should be made first as a "base" and the non-cream ones are then added to this base. Another pointer— add only half of the water called for on the labels. Otherwise, follow directions. This will insure a richer, creamier soup. Cream soup combos should be dressed up with a sprig of something like parsley or sprinkled very lightly with paprika or fresh ground pepper.

When playing with non-cream soups, let your imagination be your guide. All of my kids like vegetable beef mixed with vegetable. For some reason, this soup mixture tastes rather homemade. You can add to the illusion by tossing in a few left-over cooked vegetables. It doesn't matter what they are— even cabbage will do. If you really want to impress folks, add a few small, cooked, whole onions (you can buy them in a can).

There is something exotic about finding a whole anything in soup. Just remember to add only half the water called for on the labels.

One more pointer. Almost any of the cream soups will go well together, such as cream of chicken with cream of celery. The flavor is totally different than you'd expect. If you do blow it and create a "peculiar" tasting mix, you can sometimes salvage it by adding a little granular bouillon, either chicken or beef. Don't be afraid of adding bits of cooked chicken or turkey to your cream soups. Even vegetables are OK. If you are expecting company, try adding a small can of new, baby carrots to cream of chicken soup. Tell them that you got it at a local delicatessen that is famous for its cream soups. No one will be the wiser.

SANDWICHES

Sandwiches? In a cookbook? Of course. Remember that this book is designed for your basic incompetent cook. Sure, anybody can slap some stuff between two pieces of bread and call it a sandwich, but will anybody who is not starving eat it?

Because of its general construction, there is no such thing as a "basic sandwich". A recent survey, conducted by my seven year old daughter, "Squirt," indicates that the vast majority of America's children are raised on peanut butter and jelly sandwiches. A closer look at this authoritative study shows that even with this venerable American institution, variations exist – the most serious of which involves the degree to which the peanut butter and jelly are spread over the surface of the bread. In many cases it doesn't even come close to the edges of the sandwich, thereby requiring several bites to be taken before getting to the "good stuff".

When one considers this and other basic errors in general construction, it is painfully obvious that a little coaching is needed for the creation of a decent sandwich. Therefore, no exotic recipes are included in this section— only simple candidates for the "basic" category and a few instructions on proper sandwich-making.

Basic Sandwich Construction Techniques

A well-built sandwich tends to be eaten more readily and completely than one thrown together with little thought to its ultimate demise. America's schoolyards and playgrounds are littered with half-eaten sandwiches and bread crusts. Adherence to only three basic rules will cut this waste in half.

Rule #1

For school lunches, or any sandwich that will not be eaten immediately, use frozen bread. Note that I said frozen bread, NOT frozen sandwich. There's a big difference. A frozen sandwich tends to thaw out in a soggy, unappetizing mass, especially if wrapped in plastic or put in a plastic sandwich bag. The moisture from "freeze drying" collects on the inside of the bag and then soaks the sandwich. Therefore, it is not a good idea to prepare sandwiches ahead of time and then freeze them. Avoid this common mistake if at all possible. Instead, get up a few minutes earlier and make the sandwiches with frozen BREAD. This will do several things for the sandwich; 1) If you use lettuce, the frozen bread will keep it fresh and crisp until lunch time instead of limp and wilted. 2) Helps eliminate condensed moisture and thus soggy sandwiches. (Since only the bread was frozen very little moisture is released.) 3) Keeps the entire sandwich as fresh as if it had been refrigerated. By the time lunch rolls around the bread will have thawed and the sandwich will have the taste and appearance of one freshly made.

Rule #2

Cut off the crust. Unless the sandwich is toasted, kids won't eat the crust anyway, so why waste it? Save it for other recipes in this book. Even professional caterers cut off the crust on the fancy little things they make. Do you and the kids deserve any less? Of course not, especially since it only takes a few seconds to do so. Once the crust is off, quarter the sandwiches by making two diagonal cuts. You now have four little triangles that the kids will wolf down (if the rest of it is edible). Besides, when the kids' friends see what kind of sandwiches their dad makes, you will be the talk of the neighborhood.

Rule #3

Whatever you make the sandwich out of, make sure that it covers the bread ALL THE WAY TO THE EDGES. This is the most frequently violated rule of well-built sandwich procedure. An amateur-built sandwich has a little stuff smeared or piled in the middle while a truly professional one rewards the eater with every bite. All pictures and advertising of luscious sandwiches show the good stuff sticking out from the edges. It is not necessary to go this far as, a) you are not trying to sell the sandwich and, b) you are going to cut the edges off anyway.

EGG SALAD SANDWICHES

(For immediate consumption only)

Once friends and relatives taste this egg salad recipe, they will resort to all sorts of devious methods to obtain it. Deny all requests for information and hide your cookbook. If they try to guess what you put in, agree with all hypotheses.

Six hard-boiled eggs
2 tbsp. finely chopped onion
½ cup mayonnaise/Miracle Whip salad dressing
1 tbsp. finely chopped celery
½ tsp. dry mustard
½ tsp. ground fennel
Salt and pepper

The ground fennel is the whole secret to this recipe. DO NOT LEAVE IT OUT or all you will have is plain old egg salad and anybody can make that! Boil the eggs for at least 10 minutes. (Put the eggs in cold water and start timing when the water boils.) As soon as the eggs are cooked, place them under cold, running water. This will prevent the egg yolks from turning a dark color. Chop the eggs and throw in a large bowl. Add the rest of the ingredients and mix. Salt and pepper to your own taste. As in any "Old Indian" recipe, any of the ingredients may be left out, but if you leave the eggs out, you will only have mayonnaise goop, which most people don't like. While you may serve this egg salad on any kind of bread, it is best on lightly toasted, buttered white bread.

"BALONEY" SALAD SANDWICHES

This is similar to ham salad but tastes better and costs less. It also gives you the option of using some of the new "healthful" bolognas on the market today. They make the stuff out of cows, turkey parts, dead chickens and lord knows what else. Some of this stuff is 97% fat and flavor free, while other types have garlic, pimientos, and even cheese imbedded in it. What ever type you choose is OK as we cover up the original flavor with mayonnaise and relish. This mixture can also be frozen without losing any of its texture or flavor.

1 lb. bologna
3 tbsp. sweet relish
⅓ cup mayonnaise (more or less)
1 tbsp. chopped onion (optional)

Grind or chop the bologna (in grinder, blender, or food processor. If you don't have one of these things, you can do quite nicely with a large knife or hatchet. Be sure to use your wife's best cutting board with the knife or hatchet as this will horribly mutilate its surface and cause her to buy a blender or food processor for you to borrow). Now throw everything in a large bowl and smoosh it all up. Spread on sandwich bread. Serve open-faced at parties or for company appetizers. Very good on all sorts of crackers. Place some on cheese slices and roll up, etc.

SLOPPY JOES

(Kid style)

There are 7432 ways to make Sloppy Joes, but this is the easiest.

1 lb. ground beef
1 can Campbell's tomato soup
¼ cup chopped onions
1 tsp. prepared mustard
½ tsp. salt
¼ tsp. chili powder
1 tbsp. butter

Over medium heat, cook the onions in butter until they just turn yellow. Add the ground beef and brown. Drain off the grease and add the rest of the stuff. Simmer over low heat for 8 to 10 minutes, stirring occasionally. Serve on hamburger buns that have been warmed in the oven or lightly toasted. Should make 8 to 10 sandwiches. Serve with potato chips and pickles. Great for kid parties if you don't have to clean the kids afterward.

HOT DOGS AND BEANS

Not a very elegant meal, but then again, you don't have to invite the neighborhood blue bloods to lunch EVERY day. Your kids LIKE this kind of stuff, and if you want to shine in their eyes, you'll have to make it once in a while. Besides, most of your wife's cookbooks don't feature good stuff like this, so that automatically puts you one up on her.

2 cans of pork and beans
1 12 or 16 oz. pkg. of hot dogs
4 tbsp. light brown sugar
1 tsp. dry mustard

Heat the pork and beans over medium heat in a large sauce pan. Add all the other ingredients except the hot dogs. Stir gently but thoroughly until the brown sugar is completely mixed in with no lumps. Cut the hot dogs into bite-sized pieces and add to the pot. Reduce heat and simmer for about 15 minutes or until warmed through. Do not skimp on the hot dogs. That's the part the kids like best. Even if your wife knows about this recipe, she won't put in as many hot dogs as you do, therefore, she won't "make it as good as daddy does". A minor victory, perhaps, but a victory nonetheless.

CATHOLIC FOOD

Usually I can't stand fish unless it's fresh caught trout or bass. There will come a time, however, when you are called upon to cook the "fish" that your wife brought home from the store. Normally, it's perch, flounder, or cod (whatever is on "sale"). It really doesn't make any difference though, as it's still fish and tastes pretty much the same – like fish. People don't mind if beef tastes "beefy" or if chicken tastes like chicken, but if fish tastes like fish, it ain't good. In fact, people rate how good fish tastes by how little it tastes like fish. The less it tastes like fish the better it is! I can hear them now, "Gee, this is pretty good, doesn't taste like fish at all." I don't know why people buy the stuff in the first place. I guess it's supposed to be healthful, but then again, so are turnips.

Fish fillets
Lemons
Large onion
Butter

Wash the fish fillets under running water and pat dry with paper towels. Arrange in single layer on a large sheet of aluminum foil. Smear a little butter on the bottom of each fillet and dot the top with at least one tablespoon of butter. Cover each piece of fish with slices of lemon. Now put large slices of onion on top of each fillet (don't worry about the "onion" taste – it won't be there). Wrap the remaining foil tightly around the fish and seal the edges by folding several times. Bake in a pre-heated 350 degree oven for 20 to 25 minutes or until fish just begins to "flake". When done, remove all the onion, but serve with the lemon slices still on. Tastes great, even for fish!

To offset the healthfulness of the fillets, serve with

something like French fries or pre-cooked potato slices that are quickly fried in deep fat. A light salad will help guests digest the potatoes with less guilt.

COMPANY STUFF

Eventually you are going to want to show off your new-found cooking skills (and, hopefully, sell a few cookbooks). This is the recipe with which to do it. It not only looks good and tastes good, but it cuts down on the number of serving dishes that your wife has to wash. Everyone will appreciate your thoughtfulness.

1½ boneless chicken breasts for each moocher
1 cup cooked rice for each
1 can asparagus per four people
1 can Campbell's cheese soup
1 can Campbell's Golden Mushroom Soup
Salt and pepper
Tarragon

Wash the chicken breasts under running water, dry with paper towels and place on broiler pan. Brush with melted butter and sprinkle LIGHTLY with salt and pepper and tarragon. Broil six inches from heat for about 10 minutes on each side or until lightly browned. Baste with butter several times while broiling.

Cook rice (either instant or regular) according to instructions. If for some reason the rice should come out gooey or sticky, rinse it in a colander under running water and then reheat it either in the microwave or by pouring boiling water over it while it is still in the colander.

Heat the canned asparagus (if you are a purist, use frozen or fresh) and line a large oval serving platter with the tips of the asparagus pointing outward and just touching the edges of the platter. Add the rice to the center of the dish, covering the base of the asparagus so that only 2 or 3 inches remain uncovered. Now place your cooked chicken breasts on top of the rice in a straight line. Pour the heated Golden Mushroom soup (undiluted) over the chicken and rice. Pour the heated, undiluted cheese soup around the edge of the platter on the asparagus.

You now have a very attractive, one-dish fancy meal. Use your own judgment on how much of the "sauces" you should pour on the platter. Use just enough to make it look attractive. Put the rest in gravy boats, one on each end of the table. Most guests will recognize the Golden Mushroom Soup, but somehow it won't taste quite the same. When asked, "Is this just Golden Mushroom Soup?," tell them that you started with it due to time constraints, but that you added a host of spices and seasonings. Ask if they can tell exactly what you used. You'll be surprised at the answers. Just smile in your best condescending manner and recommend this book.

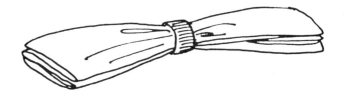

G I D CASSEROLE

(Gastrointestinal Distress)

I picked this recipe up in Alabama while teaching Army pilots how to fly helicopters on instruments. I had a student who was so uncoordinated that he could barely keep the aircraft right-side up (I suppose that's why the army decided to make him a helicopter pilot), but, boy, could he cook! (I suppose that's why the Army decided not to make him a cook). If I remember correctly, he was from a little town in "Loooose-e-ana" where his grandfather taught him how to cook. I think he's a big-wig in Army aviation now.

1½ lbs. ground beef
2 cans golden hominy
3 8 oz. cans tomato sauce
¾ lb. longhorn or mild cheddar cheese
½ cup chopped onion
Salt and pepper
Paprika
Garlic powder
Oregano
Cumin

Brown the meat and onions in a large frying pan. Have one of the kids grate the cheese. When the hamburger is cooked, drain the grease and add the tomato sauce and seasonings. Don't skimp on the seasonings. Add a LOT of everything except salt and pepper.

In a medium sized casserole dish, place successive

layers of hominy, meat mixture, and cheese, in that order, until you run out of stuff. Plan it so that you end up with the cheese on top. Bake in a pre-heated 350 degree oven for about 25 minutes or until the cheese is completely melted. I guarantee you've probably, maybe, never tasted anything quite like this. It's really good.

ROAST CHICKEN

This is a real sleeper. Easy to make and hard to screw up. This is the meal that will establish your reputation as a phenomenal cook and dispel any lingering doubt about your ability to transform ordinary food into a banquet.

1 large frying chicken (whole)
Bread crusts
Chicken bouillon
Sage
Salt and pepper
2 tbsp. finely chopped onion
Poultry seasoning

The key to this recipe is the large FRYING chicken and the bouillon. Most people buy roasting chickens to roast. A roasting chicken is nothing more than a tough, OLD, bird that managed to escape the hatchet for a number of years until its luck ran out. They require longer cooking times and are not as juicy as fryers.

Women buy roasting chickens to roast, fryers to fry, stewing chickens to stew, etc. I think it has something to do with word association. As an "Old Indian" cook, do not fall into this trap. Always buy FRYING chickens.

I like this meal because it requires very little effort and dirties only one bowl (for mixing the stuffing — this is where you use all those little bread crusts that you've been cutting off the kids' sandwiches). You don't even have to cut up the chicken. Just wash and fill with stuffing. Cut off any part of the little beastie that doesn't look edible (globs of fat, folds of skin, wing tips, etc. Leave the skin at the large opening of the chicken, however, as you will need this to hold the stuffing in.) Cut off the neck also, but throw it away.

Note: *Most women save chicken necks and other unidentifiable parts of the deceased bird by putting them in little plastic bags. The bags full of body parts are placed in the freezer for 3 or 4 months and then thrown away. Females always say that they are going to "make something" out of them, but they never do. They just keep freezing them and throwing them away. I think this is some kind of secret ritual, but I'm not sure. I once made the mistake of asking my wife about it, but all she did was give me that look that women give you when they can't find a knife. At any rate, throw the stuff away.*

Now that your chicken is washed and trimmed, it's ready to be stuffed. This is where the only bowl that has to be washed comes in. Chop about 3½ to 4 cups of the bread crusts that you've been saving into ½ inch pieces (or use seven slices of dry bread) and toss into the bowl. Cook the onion in a little butter until it turns yellow and add this to the bowl. If you want to add a little finely chopped celery to the dressing, cook it with the onions.

Now add about a half cup of water to the bowl (less if you like dryer stuffing, more if you prefer it real moist). Sprinkle ½ tsp. poultry seasoning, ½ tsp. ground sage, and a little salt and pepper over the bread crumbs. Add one heaping tsp. of instant (granular) chicken bouillon and begin smooshing it all up. If you don't have instant bouillon, use a couple of bouillon cubes, crumbled and dissolved in the water. Do a very thorough mixing job and then stuff it inside the chicken. You'll probably have a little dressing left over but just put it in an oven-safe dish and cook it along with the chicken.

Next comes the tough part — sewing up the chicken so the dressing stays inside. Women usually use thread or light string, but they're good at this type of work and I'm not. I use a couple of welding clamps, which is quick and effective. Large, spring-loaded paper clips work well too. I even know a guy that uses vise grips. What ever you use, just remember that it is going to be HOT when you take it out of the oven.

Place the bird in a shallow roasting pan and cook the whole affair, uncovered, in a preheated 375 degree oven for approximately 1½ hours. You can tell if the chicken is done by squeezing the thickest part of the drumstick (protect your fingers with paper towels). It should be very soft and the drumstick should twist easily in its socket. Start checking the bird about 15 minutes before the approximate time is up.

Throughout the roasting cycle, you should baste (brush or smear) the creature with melted butter about once every twenty minutes. After you do this a couple of times, you won't have to melt any more butter as you can use the drippings in the bottom of the pan. The chicken should be a nice golden brown color and the kitchen should smell nice and "homey." Great for a cold wintery day.

Take the stuffing out of the bird and put it in a separate bowl. The chicken should stand for about 10 to 15 minutes before carving. Use this time to make gravy from the drippings in the pan. There will be about ½ to ¾ of a cup to play with. Add a cup of water and place the pan on the top of the stove over medium heat. Put 3 or 4 tablespoons of flour and a half tsp. chicken bouillon in a jar with about a cup of milk. Screw on the lid and shake until the flour is blended. Slowly pour this into the drippings in the pan, stirring all the time. Cook until bubbly and thick. Keep stirring. Should it get too thick, add a little water to get the consistency you want. If you have a blender or even a mixer, use it on the gravy to make it super smooth and creamy.

Serve with boiled or mashed potatoes (instant potatoes work well), and one of the vegetables in this cookbook. Everyone will marvel at your ability. Accept all compliments graciously.

Note: *This recipe seems long and complicated but it really isn't. Actual "hands on" time is only about 20 minutes, including the basting. Don't get scared off as it's really an easy meal to make.*

TARRAGON CHICKEN

If you ask my children, they'll tell you that this recipe was handed down to me from "Stinky Feet," a minor Indian chief of little consequence and even less importance. The only memorable

things about this nonentity were his eating habits — and they were atrocious. It would seem that our chief liked to eat only once every three or four days. By this time, he was ravenous and what few table manners the old boy had went out the tepee flap. Mountain men were not known for their table manners either, but even these stalwarts of the "eat with the hands" school of etiquette were appalled at the chief's gluttonous eating habits and mannerisms. Therefore, in keeping with tradition, and in honor of Stinky Feet, tarragon chicken may only be eaten with the hands. No exceptions to this rule are permitted.

1 cut-up chicken for each 4 people
Cooking oil
Salt and pepper
Garlic powder
Tarragon

Over a large bowl, coat each piece of chicken with oil. Sprinkle each piece lightly with garlic powder and heavily with tarragon, salt and pepper. Place on broiler pan (covered with aluminum foil so your wife doesn't have to work so hard to clean it — she'll appreciate the thought) and put it in the oven so that the top of the chicken is about 4 or 5 inches from the broiler element (the upper one). Broil for about 10 to 12 minutes on a side or until golden brown. You may have to brush a little more oil/garlic/tarragon mixture on the chicken pieces if they start to burn on the edges before being cooked all the way through.

This is one of the absolute best ways to cook chicken. Most people have never heard of tarragon but will gobble the chicken down. This will allow you a certain amount of malignant satisfaction as you watch them turn into animals eating your creation. Remember, it MUST be eaten with the hands!

PAN FRIED ROUND STEAK

I know. It's tough. Tastes like I would imagine well worn shoe leather would. However, it is cheaper than most other cuts and sometimes it's on sale for less than hamburger. Therefore your wife probably buys it but never cooks it like a steak SHOULD be cooked. Most likely it's gooped up with soups, tomatoes, sauces, and lord knows what else. But you just don't fry or grill it like other, more tender steaks — until now, that is. Your standard of living won't go up because you tried this recipe, but your standard of eating certainly will. Purchase a good cut of bottom round about ½ inch thick and we'll take it from there. To make this type of steak tender, and actually succulent, we have to use something called a marinade. Don't quit me now, as you are about to learn how to turn shoe leather into juicy steak. It's really easy.

1½ to 2 lbs. boneless round steak
Secret "Old Indian" marinade
White pepper
Instant beef bouillon
Butter
Chives

The secret to this recipe is the secret "Old Indian" marinade. Like all marinades, its purpose is to break down the tough fibers of the meat. This is done by the acids in the solution, usually provided by the wine. In this case, we use Burgundy, but most red wines that aren't too sweet will do. The wine not only helps tenderize the meat, but adds a totally different flavor. The marinade will also enchance the natural juiciness of any cut. Don't worry about the meat tasting like an old wino smells. It won't. One little tip: don't use a plastic bowl for this. Glass or stainless steel will ensure that the meat doesn't pick up flavors other than the marinade.

Secret "Old Indian" Marinade

2 cups Burgundy
1 cup oil (preferably olive)
1½ tbsp. chopped parsley
¼ tsp. thyme
¼ tsp. tarragon
2 bay leaves

Dump all the stuff in the bowl that you intend to marinate the beef in. Mix VERY thoroughly and add the steak (cut into serving size portions and trimmed). Refrigerate for 12 hours or longer, turning meat several times. Drain the steaks but save the marinade. You can use it over and over. Melt about ¼ cup butter in a large frying pan over medium high heat. Add the steaks when the butter is nice and bubbly and cook for about 30 seconds on each side. Reduce the heat to low and cook for another 2 minutes on each side.

While this is going on, add 1 teaspoon of instant beef bouillon to several tablespoons of the marinade, stir well and pour over the steaks. Allow to cook for another minute. They should be medium rare. Remove from pan and serve immediately. Sprinkle lightly with white pepper (fresh ground pepper will do) and top with a tablespoon of butter mixed with chives. Nobody will believe that they are eating round steak — it's too flavorful and juicy. Your fame is now assured.

Note: *You can grill these marinated steaks over hot coals and get the same juicy results. Brush a little butter on them and don't over cook.*

ETHNIC FOOD

Technically, every recipe in this book is "ethnic," but this one is more "ethnic" than the others simply because it's not like anything else you've ever tasted. It's spicy, different, and delicious, not unlike Creole cooking, but it is definitely not Creole. Since its ethnogeny is unknown, we'll just call it "ethnic food" and let it go at that.

> **2 pkgs. Polish "kielbasa," about 2 lbs. (or something similar)**
> **4 itty-bitty cans tomato sauce (32 ozs.)**
> **¾ cup chopped green pepper**
> **¾ cup chopped onion**
> **3 or 4 green onions, chopped**
> **1 clove garlic**
> **2½ tsp. parsley flakes**
> **1 bay leaf**
> **Salt and pepper**
> **¼ tsp. cayenne pepper**
> **½ stalk finely chopped celery**
> **1 tsp. basil**
> **1 tsp. thyme**
> **1 cup water**

Lightly "saute" (cook in some butter) the green onion, celery, and onions in a large pan. Now add everything else except the kielbasa and stir occasionally over medium-low heat. Peel the skin off the kielbasa (or whatever sausage you decide to use), cut into big bite-sized chunks and add to the pot. Cook, stirring often, for one hour. You may have to turn the heat down to keep things from boiling. You want just enough heat to keep it below that level. Serve steaming hot. I suggest buttered new potatoes with parsley, corn-on-the-cob, and fresh-from-the-oven bread. Marvelous and different.

SCRAMBLED UP EGGS

A recipe for scrambled eggs? You bet. These are probably the finest scrambled eggs in the world. Consider yourself fortunate that I decided to include this secret recipe. People will do horrible things to your body to find out how to make these creamy smooth eggs. Do not reveal the secret.

Some eggs (two per person)
Hot sauce
Grated mild longhorn cheese
Butter

Beat the eggs thoroughly in a large bowl (best results being obtained if one removes the shells first). Add one drop of hot sauce for each egg.

Note: *You will not taste the hot sauce. All it does is enhance the flavor of the eggs.*

Add salt and pepper and beat until the mixture is smooth and consistent. You may use a fork, beater, mixer, or your drill.

Over medium heat melt two tbsp. butter in your frying pan for each 4 eggs you intend to scramble. When the butter begins to bubble, pour the eggs into the pan and IMMEDIATELY add one teaspoon of grated cheese to the pan for each egg. Slowly stir the eggs so that they do not stick to the bottom of the pan or cook more in one spot than another. Keep em moving. Remember that eggs continue to cook AFTER you remove them from the pan, so take them out a little early and serve immediately. Nobody will taste the cheese or hot sauce, but will marvel at the smoothness and flavor of your eggs.

SOFT BOILED EGGS

Soft boiled eggs are usually too soft or too hard. There is only one known way to make them perfect every time. This is it.

Some eggs
Some water

Place eggs in pan and cover with COLD water. Bring to a boil as rapidly as possible. Now here is the tricky part: For up to 3 eggs, remove pan from heat and let stand for 3 minutes. Immediately place pan (eggs and all) under cold running water to cool the eggs. For more than 3 eggs, DON'T remove from stove but reduce heat to low and let stand for an additional 30 seconds for each extra egg. If you are cooking 6 eggs, for instance, you would bring them to a boil and then immediately reduce the heat to low and let cook for 4½ minutes. For 8 eggs, it would be 5½ minutes, and so on. This works well

up to 9 eggs, after which number you should get another pot. You may have to vary this formula by a few seconds for each 1000 feet of altitude above sea level (longer) but you will still be in the ball park.

PERFECT POACHED EGGS

These can be served on lightly toasted English muffins, toast, or just plain. Some cooks will add various flavorings to the cooking water such as beef or chicken bouillon.

Some eggs
Some water

Bring water to a boil in pan or anything with a bottom and sides that is reasonably watertight and fireproof. Break eggshells and put eggs in cup or small bowl. This prevents eggs with broken yolks from getting in the cooking water. Nobody likes a poached egg with the yolk broken and waterlogged. Throw away the ones with broken yolks (unless your wife is watching, in which case refer to directions concerning egg yolks in the spinach souffle recipe).

Pour the perfect eggs into the boiling water and remove pan from heat. Let stand for four to five minutes and then remove and serve immediately. Remember, eggs continue to cook even after being

removed from the cooking medium. You should now have perfect poached eggs. For more than 5 eggs, leave the pan on the heat after adding the eggs, but reduce the fire to low. Use the same time. Again, altitude may require a few more seconds per thousand feet per egg. Experiment.

MOUNTAIN MAN PANCAKES

These pancakes are the basis of my kids' favorite breakfast. Actually they're closer to French crepes than pancakes, but "Old Indian" cooks NEVER cook dainty French stuff. If they do, they call it something else, such as "Mountain Man Pancakes." Use any name you want to avoid the social stigma attached to cooking "lacy" or "fluff stuff." REAL cooks will rise to great heights of creativity to cover up the "light" or "healthful" aspects of their products. After all, we're involved with "Old Indian" cooking, not dainty, "charming little dishes."

The beauty of this recipe is that each kid can "personalize" his own mountain man pancakes, thereby destroying any vestige or trace of social degeneration that may have inadvertantly crept into your cooking. When the kids are through, no two crepes, oops, mountain man pancakes, are exactly the same, and none would be headline fare in the Sunday food column. Tis a noble thing you do, my friend, noble indeed.

1 cup flour
¼ cup sugar
3 eggs
1 cup milk
½ tsp. vanilla
2 tbsp. melted butter
Some salt

Unfortunately, you'll need two bowls for this one, but it's worth it. In one bowl, dump the flour, sugar, and salt and mix it up (some people sift it, but what the hell). In the other bowl, beat the eggs until they're nice and thick. This usually takes 2 or 3 minutes with the mixer on medium or 1 minute in a blender on low (thirty seconds with the drill and coat hanger). Add the butter, vanilla, and milk to the eggs, stir thoroughly and dump the whole thing into the flour mixture. Blend until smooth.

Now comes the tricky part — the cooking. If your wife has a crepe or omelet pan and you are allowed to use it, do so, otherwise use a medium sized frying pan. Thoroughly butter the pan and set over medium-low heat. When the butter begins to bubble, add just enough of your batter to form a thin layer in the pan. Allow to cook until the batter appears to be "set" and the edge is dry. Now try to loosen the damn thing without tearing it and then flip it over. Most of the time a knife or spatula can be worked under the pancake successfully. Cook on the reverse side for 10 or 12 seconds only, then remove from the pan onto a large "playpen" plate. This is the plate where you or the kids will smear the whole thing with either sugar, jelly, preserves, etc., and then ROLL it up. Delicious eaten with fingers or fork. Try lots of different toppings.

If you are serving a fancy breakfast to guests, make a whole plate of rolled up mountain man pancakes stuffed with different preserves and sprinkled with powdered sugar or doused with whipped cream. The women will remark about how lucky your wife is to have you, and the men will be too busy stuffing their faces to show their grudging envy. Since this recipe only makes 15 to 20 pancakes, make a second batch. Keep them warm in a 200 degree oven until ready to serve (don't put the whipped cream on until AFTER they come out of the oven).

TIMBER THIEF POTATO BREAD

It seems like every cookbook has several recipes for making bread, which is dumb because you can buy some pretty good freshly baked stuff at the store. Besides, good bread is both hard to make and time-consuming. There will come a time, however, when your lofty status as an "Old Indian" cook will come into question if you can't produce a decent loaf of bread. This recipe will not only help remedy that situation but will cure you, once and for all, from ever wanting to try it again. I'm not against baking, mind you, I just have better things to do with my time. In fact, I consider baking bread at home to be in the same category as toilet training the kids — something best left to your wife.

I got this formula from an old geezer who lives in the "Yaak" area of extreme northwestern Montana. He gave it to me on the condition that I didn't give it to anyone else. I include it here not only because it makes damn good bread, but because you PAID for it, which, I suppose, is in keeping with the intent, if not the spirit of my agreement with the old thief. The keen observer will notice the word "potato" in the name of this bread. That's because it contains potatoes and that's also what makes it a little on the "heavy" side. If you're looking for French-type puff pastry, this isn't it. Instead, it's the kind of stuff that kept lumber jacks in the woods all day and kept the camp cook from being skinned alive. Tastes best if the potato is stolen from your neighbor's garden.

1 cup mashed potatoes (instant or real)
8 cups flour
3 eggs, beaten
1 cup scalded milk*
2 pkgs. dry yeast
¼ cup sugar
½ cup shortening
2 tsp. salt
4 tsp. melted butter

Place mashed potatoes in large bowl. Add the milk, shortening, salt, and sugar and mix thoroughly. Place in refrigerator until lukewarm. Combine the yeast with ½ cup WARM water and stir until dissolved. Add the eggs and the yeast water to the bowl and mix well. Throw in about a cup and a half of the flour and mix it in very thoroughly. Let stand in a warm place for about 30 minutes or until it starts to get pretty bubbly. This is caused by the little yeast beasties gorging themselves and making gas. Don't worry though, as this is the only time such activity is socially acceptable.

Now add 6 cups of the flour to the bowl, one cup at a time and work it in. The remaining flour should be spread on a cutting board (or counter top) and the ball of dough from the bowl placed on this. Knead the dough for at least 10 minutes (kneading is a process whereby one grabs the dough with both hands and sort of "squishes" it. You can also push down on it with the palms of both hands, turn it over, push down, turn over, push down, etc. Personally, I get great pleasure from trying to strangle the stuff by squeezing its imaginary neck and swearing that I'll never do this again.) The longer you knead the dough, the lighter the bread will be.

Set the dough aside for about 30 minutes and let it rise until it doubles in size. Repeat the kneading process all over again, only this time when you're through punching the stuff around, divide it in half and dump each part into a greased 9 x 5 loaf pan. Set the pans aside for about 30 minutes or until the dough doubles in size. Brush the top of each with melted butter and place the pans in a preheated 350 degree oven for about 45 minutes or until golden brown. About fifteen minutes before the baking time is up, brush the top again with butter. Let cool on a wire rack so that air can circulate under the bread or the bottom will "sweat".

By this time, the smell of the baking bread will have drawn every freeloader in the neighborhood to your back door. If you want to taste your own bread, do so before you let them in. Serve nice thick slices with plenty of butter and jam. Don't do this again

unless you're a glutton for punishment. It's easier to marry a baker.

"Scalded" means to bring the milk to a point just short of boiling. How do you tell if the milk is about to boil without actually letting it start to boil? I really don't know, so I usually just let a couple of bubbles pop up and then remove it quickly from the heat. I don't know if this is right or wrong, but it hasn't caused any catastrophic failures yet.

CINNAMON RAISIN NUT BREAD

If you haven't learned your lesson about baking bread from the previous recipe, try this one. It's guaranteed to send you to the store for the next loaf. This DOES produce a very good bread, but the work involved is ridiculous. "Old Indian" cooking is supposed to be fast and easy, not hot and hard. Still, this will add one more item to the list of things that your kids can brag about (especially if you're only an accountant).

7 cups flour
1 cup raisins
4 tbsp. cinnamon
4 tbsp. chopped walnuts (or pecans)
¾ cup sugar
1 cup cold water
1 cup scalded milk
2 tbsp. butter
1 tsp. salt
2 pkgs. dry yeast
¼ cup warm water

Soften the yeast in the warm water. In a large bowl, pour the scalded milk over the sugar, salt, cinnamon, and butter. Add the cold water and cool the mixture until lukewarm (if it's too warm, you will kill the yeast beasties.) Add the yeast water, mix, and add enough of the flour to make a thick paste. Keep working more flour in until all of it is gone. Add the raisins and nuts and work into the dough as you knead it. Continue kneading for at least five minutes. Let the dough stand in a warm place until it doubles in size.

Place dough on a floured board or countertop and knead again for at least five more minutes. Divide the dough in half and place in two 9 x 5 loaf pans, allowing it to double again. Brush the tops of each loaf with a little melted butter and place in a preheated 350 degree oven for about 45 minutes.

If you want to get real fancy, make a powdered sugar and milk mixture just thick enough so that it will barely pour. About a half a cup will do. 10 minutes before the bread is done, pour half of the sugar/milk mix over each loaf. It makes a neat glaze and adds to the flavor of the bread. You won't have to put a gun to anybody's head to get them to try this one! Great served hot, cold, or as toast.

OLD-FASHIONED RAISIN BISCUITS

Some of the truly fine things in life are old-fashioned— Stutz Bearcats, Parker shotguns, and, in this case, raisin biscuits. With very little shame, I freely admit stealing this recipe from my grandmother. Extremely fast and easy to make, you'll get rave reviews every time you serve them. Refuse all requests for this stolen recipe as two wrongs don't make a right.

2 cups "sifted" flour
4 tsp. baking powder
½ cup sugar
½ cup warm butter
1 cup raisins
⅜ cup milk
½ cup cream
½ tsp. salt

Sift the flour, baking powder, sugar and salt into a large bowl (actually, just dump and stir it up). Now mix in the butter with your hands and add the raisins, milk, and cream. Keep mixing until the dough forms a ball and leaves the sides of the bowl. Dump the dough out onto a floured board and flatten until it is about ⅓ of an inch thick. Any less than that and the biscuits will be too crispy on the outside. Any more than that and they won't cook properly, so try to get it as close to a third of an inch as possible.

Cut the biscuits out with a 2 inch biscuit cutter or jar lid (or pocket knife). Bake 10 to 15 minutes in a preheated hot (425 degree) oven. This should make about eighteen tender and flaky biscuits. Serve hot with plenty of butter. Don't worry about cholesterol or heart attacks, because if you have to choose a way to go, this is one of the best ways to do it.

FANCY DESSERT STUFF

A good recipe to use if you are trying to climb the social ladder and don't want to offend anybody. It's almost impossible to serve something that everybody will like. Fat people are usually on one wacky diet or another, and skinny people have weird ideas about what they should eat. Us normal people will eat most anything that doesn't bite or taste bad (and the surgeon general should keep his nose out of it).

This recipe is probably healthful, definitely has eye appeal, and can be eaten by anybody with or without teeth. Besides that, it tastes good. Should you ever run across anybody who doesn't like it, rest assured that it's not your cooking. The naysayer is just "odd," or, if he/she has money, "eccentric." Don't worry about these people unless the "eccentric" is your rich old aunt who has one foot in the grave, in which case you should agree with her and state, rather loudly, that you don't know why your wife insisted on making such stuff.

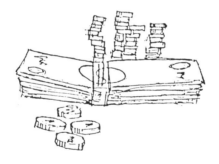

Part One — The Shells

6 eggs
¼ tsp. salt
4 tbsp. powdered sugar
¼ cup flour
2 tbsp. water

Dump the eggs, water, and salt into a large bowl and

beat thoroughly with any electric appliance that has a rotating part. Gradually add the sugar and flour and beat until smooth. Now cook as you would the pancakes in the Mountain Man Pancake recipe. This should make about ten 6 inch shells. If they should look suspiciously like crepes, dismiss the thought from your mind as they are SHELLS, not (shudder), crepes. Place the shells on individual pieces of oiled waxed paper and set aside while you work on the second half of this recipe.

Part Two — The Filling

1 10 oz. pkg. frozen red raspberries
1½ tbsp. cornstarch
1 tbsp. butter
Powdered sugar
⅓ cup Sauterne
(Or any sweet white wine)

Place the thawed raspberries, cornstarch, and sauterne in a pan and stir over medium heat. Add the butter and stir until thickened. Remove from heat. Retrieve your shells and spoon two or three heaping tablespoons of the berries on the edge of each and roll. Now arrange the rolled up shells on a platter and pour or spoon the rest of the filling down the center. Sprinkle the powdered sugar over the dessert just before serving. Marvelous.

JENNY'S PARTY COOKIES

There comes a time in every little girl's life when she has to make cookies for a special occasion, and I don't mean "cold" cookies, but real, honest-to-goodness, oven baked cookies. Following in her mother's footsteps by frantically thumbing through a half dozen cookbooks 10 minutes before she has to start cooking is probably in keeping with "the system" women have evolved over the last millenium, but hardly the most efficient.

This is where providing a little adult supervision to the females in your life can reap huge rewards. Of course, you'll have to be subtle in providing this guidance and still be able to reach your twin goals of a) teaching your children how to make cookies, and b) getting your wife to clean up the mess. Artifice is called for as wives tend to get a little surly if they even SUSPECT that you are trying to supervise them.

Try suggesting to your wife that she spend a little more time with the kids, then suggest to your child(ren) that mom "feels lonesome" and that maybe she would feel a little better if they "did something" together. Next, you slip this recipe under their little noses and wonder aloud if it's any good. If your kids are a little dense, and don't get the message right away, say that it might be nice if they and their mom go into the kitchen and bake a batch of cookies. Since you've "set them up," so to speak, the kitchen will soon be humming with activity and the smell of freshly baked cookies for you to enjoy.

Don't hover around the kitchen while they're working, as this will give the appearance of supervision, which you want to avoid. Instead, make a few appearances, bestow compliments, and smile a lot. Before you know it, they'll be asking you to taste this, taste that, and what you think of such and such. Answer all questions in a positive manner and offer an appropriate suggestion or two. Before they know what hit them, THEY will have placed you in a supervisory position. Accept this new role in the kitchen as if it were natural. Remember, this could lead to bigger and better things!

2 cups flour
1 cup butter
1 cup chopped pecans
½ cup sugar
3 tsp. water
2 tsp. vanilla

Mix the butter and sugar together until creamy and smooth. Add the water and vanilla and mix thoroughly. Add the flour a half cup at a time and blend in until all the flour is used. Add the nuts and mix until they are evenly distributed through the mixture. Now shape the dough into little "finger bars" about 1½ times the diameter of your thumb and 3 inches long. Place on an ungreased cookie sheet (rectangular pan with very low sides) and bake for about 18 minutes in a preheated 325 degree oven. Let cool just enough so that you can handle them and then roll in powdered sugar. Absolutely delicious!

KATIE'S CHOCOLATE COOKIE DELIGHT

I stole this recipe from my 7 year old daughter, Squirt (Katie), who got it from her mom, who got it from HER mom, who probably stole it. This just goes to show how low I'll sink to present good recipes in this cookbook.

3 cups flour
1 cup sugar
½ cup brown sugar
⅔ cup cocoa
2 eggs
1 tsp. vanilla
1 cup shortening
1 tsp. soda
1 tsp. salt
Marshmallows

Stir together the flour, cocoa, soda, and salt. Set aside. Add the sugar and brown sugar to the shortening and "cream" well (blend until smooth). Now add the eggs and vanilla to the sugar blend and mix well. Stir in the dry ingredients and mix very thoroughly. Shape a rounded (heaped) teaspoon of dough around ¼ of a large marshmallow or 2 small marshmallows. What you should have now is a little rounded dough ball with some marshmallow in the center.

Place on a greased cookie sheet and bake at 400 degrees until the cookies crack, about 5 to 7 minutes. Remove from the cookie sheet VERY gently, one at a time or they will fall apart. After they cool, they will not be so fragile and can be treated with less dignity.

Makes about 5 dozen. Prepare yourself for an orgy of gluttonous cookie-eating.

RICE PUDDING

This is one of those things that everybody will eat when it's put in front of them but that nobody makes anymore. Everybody's mother USED to make it, but only because she wanted to get rid of the left-over rice in the fridge. Nowadays most of the rice that is consumed in this country is in TV dinners and restaurants, ergo, no left-over rice. This recipe assumes that you hunger for the "good ole days" and would like to re-create a little of it in the kitchen. Your kids will be able to help make the kind of food that "daddy used to eat" and maybe bridge the generation gap for a little while. Since you probably don't have any left-over rice in the fridge, we'll start from scratch. You'll need:

1 cup uncooked (not instant) rice
8 tbsp. butter
1 cup sugar
1 qt. milk
1½ tsp. vanilla
¾ cup raisins
5 beaten eggs
2 tsp. cinnamon
Several stories of childhood deprivation

Put the rice and milk in a pan for which you have a cover. Bring to a boil, cover, and cook over low heat until rice is tender. Add everything else, mix thoroughly, and pour into a 2 or 2½ quart casserole dish. Bake in a preheated 350 degree oven for about 25 minutes. Serve by heaping it up in small bowls, pouring some cream (or melted vanilla ice cream) around the edges and sprinkling a little cinnamon and sugar over the whole mess. Excellent either hot or cold. Careful though, or the kids will think that you didn't have it as bad as you let on.

BUMPER'S BLENDER CHERRY SHAKES

As the name would suggest, this yummy dish was invented by a young man of rather sterling character, my 5 year-old son "Bumper." Actually he started working on this when he was only three, but didn't perfect it until he reached the ripe old age of five. This is a "secret" recipe and he only let me use it after I promised to pay him royalties.

2 cups vanilla ice cream
1 cup milk
¼ of an 8 oz. jar of maraschino cherries (with juice)

Dump everything into a blender (milk first) and blend until smooth and creamy. This is a perfect "Old Indian" recipe — simple, easy, and delicious.

Note: *Bumper suggests that you put the lid on the blender cup or you will have "Bumper's Blender Cherry Shakes" all over the kitchen. If you do forget the lid, clean up the mess right away as BBCS tends to harden into* cement in a few hours. For some odd reason, moms tend to become agitated when cherry shakes appear on the ceiling(s). Don't worry about this if you are lucky enough to already have red and white speckled ceilings–nobody will notice the cherry shake and the rancid smell will go away after several months.

OLD INDIAN PUDDING

Another recipe that is in keeping with the underlying practical and moral philosophy of this cookbook — easy, simple, and delicious. Just have your kids whip up a couple of packages of instant pudding (any kind will do) and then add a handful or two of chopped walnuts. Serve in little dishes with "instant-type" whipped cream sprayed or daubed on the top. Changes the whole flavor of the pudding and elevates it to the "fancy" category. The kids can even clean up 85 to 90 percent of the mess, which is about the best anyone can be expected to do (except wives, who have a natural tendency to be "picky").

FLAVORED WATER

This is the sort of thing that you serve on a cold winter's evening, especially with a roaring fire in the fireplace and your wife by your side (after she's done the dishes, of course). It's a good hot drink anytime that you're tired of coffee or tea and want to sleep at night (no caffeine). Each time you make it, it'll taste a little different because the measurements are very inexact (in keeping with the underlying philosophy of this book). Add a little, subtract a little, and it might not taste the same from batch to batch, but it will always be good.

Water (preferably bottled)
Cinnamon
Allspice
Nutmeg
2 or 3 cloves
Teabag(s)*
3 tsp. sugar per cup
Orange or lemon rind (optional)

Dump all the stuff in a pan and boil for about five minutes. Pour through a coffee filter into individual cups. If no filter is available, use several layers of clean cloth. Lacking that, pour VERY carefully from the pot into the cups and advise everyone NOT to drink the last half inch or so.

Note: *If your tap water is heavily chlorinated, use the bottled stuff. It doesn't cost that much. Besides the taste, the big difference is that the chlorine usually kills all the "bugs" but leaves their little bodies floating around, while in bottled water, the beasties are filtered out. Vegetarians take note.*

* One teabag is ideal for four or five cups, two is OK, but three makes it taste like flavored tea instead of flavored water. Stick with one to start. If you're some kind of health fanatic, substitute honey for the sugar.

ABOUT THE AUTHOR

Ted W. Parod, father of five, has been writing for publication for more than two decades. A commercial pilot and flight instructor with more than 9,000 flight hours in airplanes, helicopters and hot air balloons, Parod's early work combined his loves of flying and the written word. His airborne exploits have earned him the Federal Aviation Administration's Distinguished Service Award, Montana's Outstanding Pilot of the Year Award, the "Humanitarian Services" Award from Montana's Flathead County Department of Disaster and Emergency Services, and the Federal Aviation Administration's Accident Prevention Counselor of the Year Award. His aviation articles have appeared in *Air Age News*, *Journal of the Balloon Federation of America* and other publications.

After serving in the Air National Guard and U.S. Air Force and completing flight training in Nevada, Parod worked his way through college by teaching Army pilots instrument flying techniques by day, while he earned his Bachelor of Science degree, Summa Cum Laude, at night in three years.

Today, Parod lives and writes in Phoenix, Arizona. His humor columns appear in *Your Ranch Neighbor*, *The Glendale Arrow* and *The Moon Valley Arrow*. His book *Oh Oh, Daddy's Cooking!*, based on the imaginative and imagined doings of his wife, Debbie, and their children, Jennifer, Katie, Daniel, Shandy and Bobbi Lee, is warming hearts (and leftovers) in kitchens throughout the country.

Notes

Notes

Notes

Notes

Notes

This cookbook is a perfect gift for that hard-to-buy-for friend or relative. Ideal for holidays, anniversaries, weddings, birthdays or just a plain old gift for someone special.

To order extra copies, please use the order forms on the opposite page.

ORDER FORM

Use the order forms below for obtaining additional copies of this cookbook.

You may order as many copies of our cookbook as you wish for the regular price of $9.95, plus $2 postage and packing per book ordered. Mail to:

Echo Lake Press
P.O. Box 23175
Phoenix, AZ 85063

Please mail _____ copies of your cookbook @ $9.95 each plus $2 postage and packing per book ordered.
Mail books to:

Name _____

Address _____

City, State, Zip _____

You may order as many copies of our cookbook as you wish for the regular price of $9.95, plus $2 postage and packing per book ordered. Mail to:

Echo Lake Press
P.O. Box 23175
Phoenix, AZ 85063

Please mail _____ copies of your cookbook @ $9.95 each plus $2 postage and packing per book ordered.
Mail books to:

Name _____

Address _____

City, State, Zip _____